The Art of Divine Meditation

by Edmund Calamy
with chapters by C. Matthew McMahon

Copyright Information

The Art of Divine Meditation by Edmund Calamy, with chapters by C. Matthew McMahon
Edited by Therese B. McMahon

Table of Contents

Meet Edmund Calamy

Edited by C. Matthew McMahon[1]

Edmund Calamy (1600-1666) was born in London, and educated at Pembrokehall, in the University of Cambridge, where he took his degree of arts in 1619, and that of divinity in 1632. By an early discovery of his opposition to Arminianism, his fellowship was prevented, even when he was justly entitled, both by his standing, his learning, and his unblameable conversation.

The prelatical rulers in the Church of England were strongly inclined to the doctrines of Arminius at this time, and nothing could stand more in the way of preferment, to a person of Mr. Calamy's sentiments, than his publicly asserting and defending them; so that, considering his warm attachment to the Calvinistic doctrines, and his hostilities to those of the Arminian party, now basking in the beams of royal favor, Mr. Calamy had but little to expect. At last, however, he was elected *tanquam socius*, a title peculiar to Pembrokehall; which, though attended with less emolument, was at least as honorable as a fellow of the

---

[1] Taken in part from *Select Memoirs of the English and Scottish Divines*, by Thomas Smith, published by Puritan Publications, 2012.

college. Sometime after this Mr. Calamy's studious and religious character recommended him to Dr. Felton, the pious and learned bishop of Ely, who made him his domestic chaplain; and while residing in the family, paid him singular marks of affectionate regard, and at last presented him to the vicarage of Mary's in Swaffhamprior, in his own neighborhood, where he became singularly useful to his flock. Still, however, he continued in the family until the bishop's death, when he was chosen one of the lecturers of Edmund's Bury, in the county of Suffolk, where Jeremiah Burroughs was his fellow laborer. In this place he continued about ten years. Some writers have said, that during his residence in this place he was a strict conformist; but his own declaration, and that of others, affirm the contrary. It is a certain fact, that Mr. Calamy, with about thirty other worthy ministers, were driven out of bishop Wren's diocese, for not conforming to the *Visitation Articles* and the unhallowed *Book of Sports*. With these abominations he could not comply; and being in favor with the earl of Essex, he preferred him to the living of Richford, a market town in the Marches of Essex, a rectory of considerable value; but it proved ruinous to his health, and brought on a dizziness of the head, that never wholly forsook him.

Upon the death of Dr. Stoughton he was chosen minister of Mary Aldermanbury, London, in 1639. Here he soon acquired a very distinguished reputation, and made a conspicuous appearance, by the active part he took in the important controversy respecting church government, then greatly agitated.

In 1640, he was employed, with several other puritan divines, in composing that famous book, entitled, *Smectymnuus;* which is said to have given the first fatal blow to episcopacy in England. This strange title is made up of the first letters of the names of its various authors, *viz.,* Stephen Marshall, Edmund Calamy, Thomas Young, Matthew Newcomen, and William Spurstow. It was done in answer to a book, entitled, *An Humble Remonstrance,* written by the bishop of Exeter. This learned prelate attempted a confutation of *Smectymnuus;* to which the Presbyterians replied. After this, the far-famed Usher, bishop of Armagh, attacked it; but was repulsed by John Milton, the celebrated author of *Paradise Lost.* The activity, the profound knowledge, integrity, and intrepidity; evinced by Mr. Calamy, had raised his reputation, particularly among the Presbyterians, to the first rank of literary fame. He was appointed, by the House of Lords, a member of the subcommittee for accommodating ecclesiastical affairs; and shortly after this he was appointed a member of the assembly of divines. He was an active and zealous man in all their proceedings, and much distinguished, both for his learning and moderation, in the assembly.

Mr. Calamy was one of the most popular preachers in London, and frequently appointed to preach before the long parliament; for which the prelatical party had treated him with unmerited abuse. He was the first, however, who, before the committee of parliament, defended the proposition, that a bishop and presbyter, according to the scriptures, are one office under different appellations. His interest and influence in the city of London was very extensive, and he preached to a numerous and highly respectable audience, composed of the most eminent citizens, and many persons of quality. He was one of the London ministers who declared against the proceedings of the army, and the violent measures that brought on the king's death; an event which he strongly deprecated.

In Cromwell's time Calamy lived as quietly as possible; but sometimes opposed the protector's measures. It is said of Cromwell, that having a wish to put the crown on his own head, he sent for some of the principal divines of the city, as if he made it a matter of conscience, and that he wanted their advice. Mr. Calamy was one who boldly opposed the project of Cromwell's single government, offering to prove that the thing was not only unlawful, but that it was also impracticable. To the first of these Cromwell readily replied, "That the safety of the people was the supreme law; but, pray, Mr. Calamy, said he, how is it impracticable?" "Because (Mr. Calamy says) the nation will be against you, nine out of ten at least." "But (Cromwell says) what if I wrest the sword from the nine, and put it in the hands of the tenth—will not that do the business?" In 1659, Mr. Calamy concurred with the Earl of Mansfield, and other great men, in persuading general Monk to bring in the king, that an end might be put to the public confusions. He preached before the parliament the day before they voted the king's restoration to the throne, and was one of these divines that were sent over to Holland on that business; but he had, soon after, cause to regret the hand he had in that unhappy transaction, particularly that he was received without a previous treaty.

On the restoration of Charles, Mr. Calamy was encouraged to hope that considerable favor and indulgence, both to himself and his brethren would still be granted. In June, the same year, he was sworn in as chaplain to his majesty, with several other Presbyterian ministers; but none of them preached more than once before the king in that capacity. About this time Mr. Calamy was often with his majesty at Earl Mansfield, the chamberlain's lodgings, and other places, and had the royal countenance on all occasions. He had a principal hand in drawing up the proposals, at that time presented to the king, respecting church government; which led the way to the Savoy conference. He was also concerned in the concessions made by the declaration of October 25th, the same year; and being one of the commissioners, he was employed, with others, in drawing up the exceptions against the liturgy, as also the reply to the reasons of the Episcopal divines against these exceptions of the Presbyterians. In 1661 he was one of those chosen by the London ministers to represent them in the convocation; but was not permitted to sit in that assembly. He attended the several meetings at the Savoy, where he did everything in his power to affect an accommodation; but without the least effect.

Mr. Calamy preached his farewell sermon on the 17th of August 1662, a week before the act of uniformity took effect. Having consulted with his great friends at court, the following petition was drawn up, and presented to the king, signed by a considerable number of the London ministers:

"May it please your excellent majesty. Upon former experience of your majesty's tenderness and indulgence to your obedient and loyal subjects, in which number we can clearly reckon ourselves, we, some of the ministers within your city of London, who, by the late act of uniformity, are likely: to be cast out of all public service in the ministry, because we cannot, in conscience, conform in all things required in the said *Act*, have taken the boldness humbly to cast ourselves and our concernments at your majesty's feet, desiring that, of your princely wisdom and compassion, you would take some effectual course, whereby we may be continued in the exercise of our ministry, to teach your people their duty to God and your majesty; and we doubt not, but by our dutiful and peaceable carriage therein, we shall render ourselves not altogether unworthy of so great a favor." This petition was presented by Mr. Calamy, Dr. Manton, Dr. Bates, and others, on the third day after the act became in force. Mr. Calamy made a speech on the occasion, stating, that those of his persuasion were ready to contest the point of fidelity to his majesty with any description of men in England: That they little expected to be dealt with in the manner they had been; and that they were now come before his majesty, imploring his interference in their behalf, as the last application they should make. The king promised to consider their request, and the day following the matter was fully debated in council, in presence of his majesty, who was pleased to say, he intended an indulgence if it was at all possible. The mends of the silenced ministers in the council, whose hopes had been flattered with a variety of specious promises, were now permitted freely to state their reasons for not putting the act in execution; and they reasoned most strenuously on the impolicy and absurdity of the measure, and the fatal effects, to the nation at large, that must necessarily attend its execution. But Dr. Shelden, bishop of London, in an animated speech, declared, "That it was now too late to think of suspending a law which had occupied so much of the time and the wisdom of the legislature in enacting—A law, in obedience to which he had already ejected such of his clergy as would not comply with it; and were they now to be restored, after thus being exasperated, he must, in that case, expect to feel the weight of their resentment; and in place of maintaining his Episcopal authority amongst them, be subjected to their scorn and animosity, being thus countenanced by the court. Besides, should the sacred authority of this law be now suspended, it would render the legislature both ridiculous and contemptible; and should the pressing importunity of such disaffected people be considered a sufficient reason why they should be humored on this occasion, it would establish a precedent upon which all future malcontents would build their hopes, and maintain their claims to similar indulgence:—the obvious consequence of which would be, convulsions, and never ceasing distractions, both in church and state." It was, on these grounds, carried that no indulgence whatever should be granted. Mr. Calamy was offered a bishopric which he refused, because he could not obtain it on the terms of the king's declaration. He preserved his temper and moderation after his ejection, and lived much retired; but going to Alder Manbury church one day as a hearer, and the clergyman appointed to preach failing to come forward; to gratify the wishes of the people who were assembled, and prevent a disappointment, he condescended to give them a *dis coupse (discourse)*, though unpremeditated. For this he was shut up in Newgate prison, by warrant from the lord mayor, as a violator of the Act of Uniformity.

A popish lady, passing through the city, found it almost impossible to proceed through Newgate Street for the number of coaches in waiting. Surprised at this incident, curiosity led her to inquire into the occasion. Some of the bystanders informed her, that an ejected minister, greatly beloved in the city, had been imprisoned for preaching a single sermon, and his friends were calling to pay him a visit in prison. This information so struck the lady, that she waited on the king at Whitehall, and told him the whole affair, expressing her apprehension, that such steps might alienate the affection of the city from his majesty. It was partly owing to this, that Mr. Calamy was soon released by an express order from the king. This circumstance being afterwards complained of in the House of Commons, it was signified that his release was occasioned by a deficiency of the Act itself, and not by the sole orders of his majesty. The following entry was therefore made on the journal of the House: "*Die Jovis*, 1662-63. Upon complaint made to this House, that Mr. Calamy, being committed to prison upon breach of the *Act of Uniformity*, was discharged upon pretense of some defect in the act—*Resolved*, that it be referred to a committee to look into the act of uniformity as to the matter in question, and see whether the same be defective, and wherein." And shortly after this, a committee was appointed to bring in the reasons of the House for advising the king to grant no toleration, with an address to his majesty; which paved the way for all that unqualified severity, and tyrannical procedure, that followed during this and the succeeding reign.

Mr. Calamy lived to see the dreadful fire of London in 1666. This awful conflagration is said to have overrun 373 acres of ground within the walls, and to have burned down 13,200 houses, and 89 parish churches, beside chapels, and that only 11 parishes within the walls were left standing. This dreadful spectacle is said to have broken Mr. Calamy's heart. He was driven through the ruins of the city in a coach, and viewing the dreadful solitude, and far spread desolation, he went home with a heavy heart, and never after left his chamber; but died in less than a month, October 1666, in the sixty-seventh year of his age.

His works:

His works are numerous. He was one of the authors of *Smectymnuus*, formerly mentioned. He was also concerned in drawing up the *Vindication of the Presbyterial Church Government and Ministry*, and *Jus Divinum Ministerii Evangelici et Anglicani*. He has also several sermons and treatises extant, given in the following list in their original titles and punctuation:

1. A collection of several sermons preached upon solemn occasions (1659)
2. A compleat collection of farewel sermons (1663)
3. A just and necessary apology against an unjust invective (1646)
4. A patterne for all (1658)
5. A Serious advice to the citizens of London (1657)
6. A sermon preached at Aldermanberry-Church, Dec. 28. 1662. in the fore-noon, late pastor of the same congregation.
7. A sermon preached by Mr. Edmund Calamy at Aldermanbury, London, Aug. 24, 1651 (1651)
8. An answer to the articles against Master Calamy, Master Martiall, Master Burton, Master Peters, Master Moleigne, Master Case, M. Sedgwicke, M. Evans, &c. and many other divines (1642)
9. An indictment against England (1645)
10. Eli trembling for fear of the ark. A sermon preached at St. Mary Aldermanbury, Decemb. 28. 1662. (1662)
11. Englands antidote, against the plague of civil warre (1645)
12. Englands looking-glasse, presented in a sermon, preached before the Honourable House of Commons (1642)
13. Evidence for heaven containing infallible signs and reall demonstrations of our union with Christ and assurance of salvation (1657)

14. Gods free mercy to England (1642)
15. Master Edmund Calamy's leading case (1663)
16. Old Mr. Edmund Calamy's former and latter sayings upon several occasions (1674)
17. Saint memorials: or, Words fitly spoken (1674)
18. The art of divine meditation. Or, A discourse of the nature, necessity, and excellency thereof (1680)
19. The city remembrancer. Or, A sermon preached to the native-citizens, of London (1657)
20. The doctrine of the bodies fragility (1654)
21. The door of truth opened: or, A brief and true narrative of the occasion how Mr. Henry Burton came to shut himself out of the church-doors of Aldermanbury: (1645)
22. The fixed saint held forth in a farwell sermon (1662)
23. The great danger of covenant-refusing, and covenant-breaking. Presented in a sermon (1646)
24. The happinesse of those who sleep in Jesus (1662)
25. The monster of sinful self-seeking, anatomized (1655)
26. The noble-mans patterne of true and reall thankfulnesse (1643)
27. The righteous mans death lamented (1662)
28. The saints rest: or Their happy sleep in death (1651)
29. The saints transfiguration: or The body of vilenesse changed into a body of glory (1655)
30. Two solemne covenants (1647)

Mr. Calamy's oldest son was ejected at the same time with his father; and his grandson, a dissenting divine of great eminence, is well known by his learned works.

.

Godly Meditation:
A Duty for All Believers
by C. Matthew McMahon

"Finally, brethren, whatsoever things are true, whatsoever things are honest, whatsoever things are just, whatsoever things are pure, whatsoever things are lovely, whatsoever things are of good report; if there be any virtue, and if there be any praise, think on these things." (Phil. 4:8).

Consider Philippians 4:8. All of these adjectives have the duty of thinking, or meditation in common. Each of these adjectives describes the "things" we are to meditate on. This is Paul's exhortation (the Holy Spirit's *command*) to meditate on them. It is a duty which connotes a thought process of careful deliberation. People often attribute meditation to something akin to oriental mysticism. This is not what biblical meditation is about. Instead, the bible exhorts us to *ponder the word of God*. Pondering God and His works is the duty of every Christian and commanded by God for daily piety. The Reformers and Puritans believed this emphatically, and they were master exegetes at drawing God's mind on this matter out of the word of God.

What then, does it mean to meditate? Meditation will not be sweet to you until it is first understood, exercised, and then exercised with profit. You cannot know how sweet it is without doing it; and, this is not merely head knowledge of something done. It is an experience with the Savior, Jesus Christ.

Consider some thoughts on divine meditation by previous ministers and theologians of the church. Thomas Hooker said, "Meditation is a serious intention of the Mind whereby we come to search out the truth and settle it on the heart."[2]

Thomas Brooks said, "Remember, it is not hasty reading—but serious meditating upon holy and heavenly truths, that make them prove sweet and profitable to the soul. It is not the bee's touching of the flower, which gathers honey—but her abiding for a time upon the flower, which draws out the sweet. It is not he who reads most—but he who meditates most, who will prove the choicest, sweetest, wisest and strongest Christian."[3]

William Fenner said, "Meditation is a settled exercise of the mind for the further inquiry of the truth, and so affecting the heart with that, and therefore there are four things in meditation, 1) an exercise of the mind, 2) a settled exercise that dwells on the truth, 3) to make a further inquiry...meditation pulls the latch of the truth and looks into every closet, and every cupboard, and every angle of it, and 4) it labors to affect the heart."[4]

Thomas White said, "Divine meditation we may say, is a serious solemn thinking and considering of the things of God, to the end that we might understand how much they

[2] Hooker, Thomas, *The Application of Redemption*, (London: Peter Cole, 1656) 210.
[3] Brooks, Thomas, *The Works of Thomas Brooks,* Volume 1, (Edinburgh: Banner of Truth Trust, 1980) 7.
[4] Fenner, William, *The Use and Benefit of Divine Meditation*, (London: E.T. 1657) 2-3.

concern us, and that our hearts by it may be raised to some holy affections and resolutions."[5]

Thomas Watson said, "Meditation is the soul's retiring of itself, that by a serious and solemn thinking upon God, the heart may be raised up to heavenly affections."[6]

John Ball said, "To meditate, signifies primarily to meditate, commune, or discourse with one's self, or which is the same, to imagine, study, consider or muse in mind or heart. Meditation is a serious, earnest and purposed musing on some point of Christian instruction, tending to lead us forward toward the Kingdom of Heaven, and serving for our daily strengthening against the flesh, the world and the Devil. Or it is the steadfast and earnest bending of the mind on some spiritual and heavenly matter, discoursing on it with ourselves, until we bring it to some profitable point, both for the settling of our judgments, and the bettering of our hearts and lives."[7]

Nathaniel Ranew said, "Pious meditation is the duty of every Christian; or, it is the high institution of Christ, and greatly incumbent duty of Christians, to exercise themselves much in holy meditation. Meditation is of that happy influence, it makes the mind wise, the affections warm, the soul fat and flourishing, and the conversation greatly fruitful. Meditation is to be the motion of the

---

[5] White, Thomas, *Instructions for the Art of Divine Meditation*, (Coconut Creek: Puritan Publications, 2013) 22.
[6] Watson, Thomas, *The Saint's Spiritual Delight and the Christian on the Mount*, (Coconut Creek, FL: Puritan Publications, 2013) 50.
[7] Ball, John, *A Treatise of Divine Meditation*, (Crossville: Puritan Publications, 2016) 27.

heavenly spirit heavenward; to carry it up to heaven and keep it a time there: a looking of the eye of the mind, and a lifting up of the heart, a making a stay, and taking a spiritual solace in heaven with God."[8]

Richard Allestree said, "Meditation is, a serious and solemn considering of heavenly things, to the end we may understand how much it concerns us, and that our hearts thereby may be raised to some holy affections and resolutions."[9]

Thomas Manton said, "The word feedeth meditation, and meditation feedeth prayer. Meditation must follow hearing and precede prayer. What we take in by the word we digest by meditation and let out by prayer."[10]

William Bridge said, "It is the vehement or intense application of the soul unto something, whereby a man's mind doth ponder, dwell and fix upon it, for his own profit and benefit. There must be the application, of the soul to something; and therefore, sometimes it is expressed by laying of a thing to heart: "The righteous are taken away, and no man lays it to heart;" no man considers on it. "If ye will not lay these things to heart," *etc.* Mal. 2:2. And as there must be an application, so there must be a vehement and intense application of the soul unto a thing, for every

---

[8] Ranew, Nathaniel, *Solitude Improved by Divine Meditation*, (Morgan: Soli Deo Gloria, 1995) 57.
[9] Allestree, Richard, (1619-1681). *The Whole Duty of Divine Meditation Described in All Its Various Parts and Branches: With Meditations on Several Places of Scripture*, (London: Printed for John Back, 1694) 2.
[10] Manton, Thomas, *The Complete Works of Thomas Manton*, Volume 17, (Worthington, IL: Maranatha Publications, 1979) 272.

consideration does not make meditation: consideration heightened makes meditation. Meditation is the work of the whole soul. The mind acts, and the memory acts, and the affections act. "Let the words of my mouth, and the meditations of my heart:" it is an intense and a vehement application of the soul unto truth."[11]

Ezekiel Culverwell said, "Meditation is a study to get grace, whereby upon all occasions we make some good use of all that comes to our mind, whereof the frequentest use shows the most heavenly soul, as contrarily the neglect thereof the carnal."[12]

Thomas Boston said, "Meditation is a necessary duty, to the performance of which, people should set themselves; seriously making choice of such times and places for it, as the duty may be gone about with the best advantage. Meditation is to think on some spiritual thing, in order to the bettering of the heart."[13]

It is your duty to meditate. What is a *duty?* A duty is something obliged to be done. We, as Christians, are obliged to meditate *because God commands it.* Why does God command it, or, what is the end or goal of meditation? As with every duty, in fact, the whole of one's life, it is the glorification of God.[14] Secondly, it is for the edification of

---

[11] Bridge, William, *The Works of the Rev. William Bridge,* Volume 3, (Beaver Falls: Soli Deo Gloria, 1989) 125.
[12] Culverwell, Ezekiel, *Time Well Spent in Sacred Meditations,* (London: T. Coates, 1635) 216.
[13] Boston, Thomas, *The Complete Works of Thomas Boston*, Volume 4, (Wheaton: Richard Owen Roberts Publishers, 1980), Sermon 39.
[14] "Whether therefore ye eat, or drink, or whatsoever ye do, do all to the glory of God," (1 Cor. 10:31).

ourselves. God never gives us spiritual "busy work" for the sake of work. There is always a purpose for everything under the sun.[15] Thirdly, it is for the further edification of the church in various ways. *Think* about this: if we are not thinking Christians what will we neglect to do simply from a lack of thought? What duties will we forget, or what spiritual gifts will we not exercise? Who will we *not help?* Who will we *not speak with* after solemn consider of some spiritual benefit? Our personal devotional time is critical in our walk as a Christian in the church of Christ eagerly awaiting the day of His coming.[16] There should be a close watch on these ends so that we may never mistake using the duty of meditation for the glory of God, for our own profit, and for our own usefulness in the church.[17]

Meditation is not just a memorization or regurgitation of theological thoughts; we must be more than a student in this act and exercise. It should be described as "serious thought." The highest seriousness makes the best scholar, and consequently, the best Christian. This is a *searching and scanning,* a deep dive into the things of God. In Calamy's work on meditation, he shows that it should be a peculiar visit to the throne room of heaven. Would it be special to visit God's throne-room? And this is not something done once and forgotten; it is something done

---

[15] "To every thing there is a season, and a time to every purpose under the heaven," (Eccl. 3:1).

[16] "Looking for and hasting unto the coming of the day of God," (2 Peter 3:12).

[17] "Let the words of my mouth, and the meditation of my heart, be acceptable in thy sight, O LORD, my strength, and my redeemer," (Psa. 19:14).

daily. In relation to our will, it fixes it to resolve to do that which God desires. It sets us to do the things we are thinking about. It places the mind and will under the influence of the Spirit, and it helps us to avoid sin, among many other things he will point out.

There are those who make excuses not to do it, and those who neglect it totally, or even those who have never learned to do it rightly. There is a right way and wrong way to meditate or think on these things of the Lord. Serious thinking is fundamental to all right doing. Meditation is hard and difficult; in that it is an acting of the quickest faculty and the most slippery part of the soul. It is easy to let the mind go. But you cannot be a good Christian no matter what others may think of you if you neglect this or reject it because you find it too hard. You cannot be a subject of Christ if you do not submit to the Law of Christ.[18] You may have to ask yourself what sin is stopping you from engaging in such a blessed help? This is to think like a Christian.

Blessings to you in the Lord as you Meditate!
C. Matthew McMahon, Ph.D., Th.D.
From my study, September, 2019

---

[18] "And why call ye me, Lord, Lord, and do not the things which I say?" (Luke 6:46).

To the Christian Reader

The heathen moralist Plutarch said, "Meditation is as it were the recovery of decaying knowledge; because as forgetfulness seems to be the egress of knowledge, Meditation doth restore a new memory instead of that which passes away; and so preserve knowledge, that it is in effect the same, in that, notwithstanding mutations, it leaves something new, and like itself, resembling that which is Divine." In considering this, how may a Christian, endowed with the true knowledge of God, say with the Psalmist in its revival, Psalm 104:34, "My meditation of him shall be sweet." When he is alone, and has no other companions to refresh himself with, then he may (as Bishop Hall, who penned a part of his *Meditations* under the solitary Hills of Ardenna) from a renewed mind, send forth his active thoughts. These are those immediate rays of that candle of the Lord within him, to contemplate on his Maker, Savior, and Sanctifier, and reflect on himself, who is to survive the visible Creation. He raises himself into a *heaven on earth* and relishes such sweetness as the carnal mind and sensual heart, immersed in dreggy matter, and is dulled with it, is never so happy as to attain.

The author of this little *treatise*, whose great and pious soul was notably brought to heaven by the frequent exercise of holy meditation, the very same who penned The Godly Man's Ark,[19] which has been often printed for the

---

[19] Updated and republished by Puritan Publications.

support of drooping Christians, among other excellent discourses upon various subjects in the exercise of his ministry with great success, did from his own experience recommend this work of *meditation*, whether ejaculatory and occasional, or solemn and deliberate. I am not ignorant, that many other eminent Divines, people of great worth and honor, have already notably displayed the excellency and usefulness of this way of thinking; yet perhaps this grave and famous preacher in his day, has in an easier method, and plain way, by his familiar expressions and resemblances, suited to vulgar capacities, here helped the real Christian, who would most delight in the duty to put meditation into practice. It may be that Mr. Calamy has done this better than any who have gone before him. No doubt, had this excellent person himself published this discourse here presented to your view, you would have had it every way more accurate, by the lopping off some superfluities, and amending of phrases, *etc.*, more proper for a writer, than these of a preacher to a popular audience. Yet such as it is, considering the author in the pulpit, you will find when you have read it through, it fully as much resembles Mr. Calamy in his preaching at Aldermanbury, to your minds, as the engraver on the title page has represented his face to your eyes. I dare say any of you who were his hearers, will be abundantly satisfied. And though this piece is posthumous, yet it is genuine, and points to Christ through repentance and godly living, "Seeing there is joy in heaven over one sinner that repents, more than over ninety-nine just people which need no repentance," (Luke 15:7). It is the hope that

these practical sermons on meditation, taken by the swift
pen of a ready writer, have an influence on many, to bring
them to the frequent and beneficial practice in the duty of
meditation, which Calamy held as necessary. No one who
preferred things before words, and esteem real knowledge
above elegant speech, as the general good of mankind,
beyond that of any particular country, can justly think the
author wrong in his assessment. He is to be noted among
those such as Dr. Preston, Mr. Fenner, Mr. Hooker, *etc.*,
(some of whose *works* popularly delivered with plainness
on the subject were suited to the capacities of their hearers,
and taken but rudely from their mouths, more benefited
readers of less abilities, than those which while alive, they
themselves published with greater exactness). He is
renowned, when he has by this more diffusive *good work*
been any way instrumental to have God and the things of
heaven (where he now resides) more delightfully thought
on. As judicious Calvin, in his *Epistle to the King of
Swetheland* prefixed to his *commentary* on the Minor
Prophets, said he would not be so morose a censor of
manners, as to obstruct the publishing of that commentary
delivered in an extemporal kind of speaking, when designed
only for his own private oratory, not otherwise to have come
abroad. Only as it was penned from his mouth by Budaeus,
Crispin, and Ionvil, because he said, he had long before
learned not to serve the theater of the world. Otherwise, he
afterwards tells the reader, that if in his other works which
he had written deliberately and succinctly with much more
pains, he had met with envious malignants, who carped at

and quarreled them, he might well endeavor to suppress that work, taken by the aforesaid writers after him, as it was freely uttered to his own hearers for present use. Yet, when others assured him, that it would be a loss (yes, injurious) to the church, if it was not printed as it was taken, rather than not at all. He on this having no time or strength to transcribe or amend it, readily permitted it to go to the press. And the Reformed Church has since rejoiced in the benefit of having it as it was published. Yes, and to this day divines who have made great use of it since in their commentaries, as well as others, to find the true meaning of the Holy Scripture, have heartily blessed God for it. Yet as Bishop Wilkins has observed in his *Epistle* to the real character, foreigners in short-writing come far behind us here in England (though it has been now seventy years invented) where they admire the skill of our writers, and whether the divines of other nations frequently come and learn our language, chiefly to understand our practical sermons, many of which have been only preserved in this way. You have, it is to be hoped to be a very useful piece, taken well from the mouth of Mr. Edmund Calamy.

Introduction

Genesis 24:63, "And Isaac went out to meditate in the field at eventide."

It is not unknown to you, I suppose, that there are two things required by God of all those that would receive the benefit of the sacrament. The one is preparation before they come; and the other is meditation when they come. I have made *many* sermons concerning *preparation*, but I have made very few of meditation. Now the sacrament is a meditating ordinance, as I may so express myself. It is an ordinance for meditation. And the great work that we have to do at the sacrament, is to meditate on Christ crucified. Therefore, I shall crave leave to give you a few sermons concerning this rare and excellent doctrine of meditation. For this purpose, I have chosen this in Genesis, in which we have four particulars.

1. We have the person that is here spoken of, and that is Isaac, the godly child of godly Abraham.

2. What is here related of this person, he went out to meditate.

3. The place that he chose for his meditation, and that was in the field; he went out into the field to meditate.

4. The time that he chose to meditate in, and that was the evening; and Isaac went out to meditate in the field at the eventide.

The great question for the meaning of this text will be, what the subject of Isaac's meditation was? What did

Isaac go out to meditate on? Now for this you must know there is a double meditation; there is a meditation that is sinful and wicked, and there is a meditation that is holy and godly.

1. There is a meditation that is sinful and wicked, and that is when we meditate on things that are wicked. Psalm 36:4, "He deviseth mischief upon his bed." And Psalm 7:14, "Behold he travelleth with iniquity, and hath conceived mischief." There are wicked meditations as well as wicked conversations; and a man may go to hell for plotting wicked things, as well as for practicing wicked things. And therefore, it is said, Prov. 12:2, "A man of wicked devices" will God condemn. Not only a man of wicked practices, but a man of wicked devices will he condemn. There is a contemplative wickedness as well as an actual wickedness; and a man may go to hell for contemplative wickedness. As for example, there is a contemplative murder, when a man delights in the thoughts of murdering his brother; when the thought of revenge is pleasing. And there is a contemplative adultery, when a man plots how to commit adultery, and delights in the thought of adultery. Now Isaac's meditation certainly was not of things that are wicked, he did not go out into the field to meditate on vile and wicked things.

2. There is a meditation that is holy and godly, and that is when we meditate on things that are holy and heavenly; and of this nature was the meditation of Isaac. He went out into the field to meditate on the works of God, and of the blessings and mercies of God; to meditate on the heavenly Canaan, and on his sins; and this appears, because

the Hebrew word that is here used for *meditation*, that is here translated *meditation*, also signifies *to pray*, and therefore it is in the margin of your bibles, "and Isaac went out to *pray* at eventide." It was a religious work that Isaac went out about; and you must know that prayer and meditation are very well joined together. Meditation is a preparation to prayer, and prayer is a fit close for meditation. Isaac went out to meditate, to pray and to meditate, and to meditate and pray. This meditation was a holy and heavenly act of Isaac. So, then the *observation* or doctrine I shall gather is this:

DOCTRINE: That the meditation of holy and heavenly things is a work that God requires at the hands of all people. That God that requires you to pray, requires you to meditate as well as pray. Yet, there are few Christians who believe this doctrine, that God that requires you to hear sermons, and yet, requires you to meditate on the sermons you hear.

1. God requires this of you that are young gentlemen, and therefore here you read of Isaac, that he went out to meditate. Now though it is true that Isaac at this time was forty years old, yet in those days to be of forty years was to be but a young man, for Isaac lived one hundred and eighty years. Therefore, this is a notable pattern for young gentlemen, to employ their time in godly and holy meditation.

2. This is a duty that God requires of kings, of nobles, and of great people. Therefore David, though he was a king, and had a great deal of work and business, yet he says of

himself in Psalm 119:15, "I will meditate in thy precepts." Verse 23, "Princes also did sit and speak against me, but thy servant did meditate in thy statutes." Verse 48, "I will meditate in thy statutes."

3. This is a duty that God requires at the hands of soldiers, and generals, and captains. In Joshua 1:8, there God speaks to Joshua, "This book of the Law shall not depart out of thy mouth, but thou shalt meditate therein day and night, that thou mayest observe to do according to all that is written therein, for then thou shalt make thy way prosperous, and then thou shalt have good success."

4. It is a duty that God requires of all learned men, and of all those that are scholars. 1 Tim. 4:15, "Give attendance to reading and exhortations, and meditate upon these things: give thy self wholly unto them."

5. This is a duty that God requires of women. Therefore, it is said of Mary in Luke 2:19, "She kept all these sayings, and pondered them in her heart." Verse 51, "But his mother kept all these sayings in her heart," that is, she meditated on them. In a word, it is a duty that God requires of all that look for blessedness, Psalm 1:1, "Blessed is the man that walketh not in the counsel of the ungodly, nor standeth in the way of sinners, nor sitteth in the seat of the scornful, but his delight is in the Law of the Lord, and in his Law doth he meditate day and night."

Now you must know there are two sorts of Divine meditation, there is a sudden, short, occasional meditation of heavenly things; and there is a solemn, set, deliberate meditation. I shall crave leave to speak something concerning the first sort of meditation, which I call sudden and ejaculatory, extemporary and occasional meditation; and I shall show you three things concerning this.

1. I will show you what this ejaculatory and extemporary meditation of divine things is, and its excellency of it.

2. I will give you some examples of it.

3. I will give you some motives to persuade you to the practice of it.

Chapter 1:
Occasional Meditation

1. I will show you what I mean by what I call occasional and extemporary, sudden and ejaculatory meditation. Occasional meditation is this, when a man takes an occasion by what he sees, or by what he hears, or by what he tastes, anything that is sensitive, in this he raises up his thoughts to heavenly meditation. Or take it in this way, occasional meditation is when a man makes use of the creature, as a footstool to raise him up to God, as a ladder to heaven. It is when a man, all of a sudden, makes use of what he sees with his eyes, or hears with his ears, as a ladder to climb to heaven with. You have a pattern of this in Psalm 8:3-4, "When I considered thy heavens, the work of thy singers, the Moon, and the Stars, which thou hast ordained, (*mark what is his meditation of this*) what is man that thou art mindful of him? and the son of man that thou visitest him?" Lord, what is man that you should make heaven, the sun, and the moon, and the stars for his sake? You must know, that the whole creation is a picture of God; it is God's mirror in which you may behold the God of heaven and earth. There is no creature, but it has the image of God on it. There is not the least spice of grace but you that are spiritual may read God in it. It is the saying of a heathen, "Every herb that you have in your Garden represents the divinity, or nature of God." There are two books that God has given us Christians to know him by, the book of the Scripture, and the book of the creature. Now, the book of Scripture is the

better book of the two, and the book of Scripture will teach us more of God than the book of the creature. For, the book of the Creature cannot teach us God in Christ, cannot teach us the mystery of Redemption, nor the mystery of the Trinity. Yet, the book of the creature is a rare book, in which a man may learn excellent things concerning heaven and heavenly things, excellent instructions.

I remember a story of a godly man, Antony, that was driven into the wilderness for religion's sake, and having no book at all in the wilderness, he was asked, "How he could spend his time?" He says, "I have one book, and that is the book of the creation; and as long as I have this book, I lack no other book," speaking about how much he could behold God in that book. And it is a good saying of Tertullian, "The same God is the God of nature that is the God of grace." And it is the duty of a Christian to receive instruction, and spiritual benefit from natural things as well as from gracious and spiritual things, because there is the same God of nature as of grace. The creation of God itself is a divine Book in which we may read the power of God, the goodness of God, the love of God, the mercy and wisdom of God, (Rom. 1:20). Things which can be known about God may be read in the creature. Now the creatures are but spectacles by which we are enabled to read these things concerning God. I have read a story of a painter, Hermogenes, he was a rare man for that art, and coming into a painter's shop, he sees a line drawn so curiously, that he cries out, "Surely Apelles has been here; none but Apelles could draw such a curious line." And as the story says, he went out of the shop, and never left until he had found out this person Apelles, so that he might come to the acquaintance of that man that had so much skill. The application of this is most excellent. When you look on this creature of God, and that creature of God, you must necessarily confess that none, but a God could make such a glorious world; *digitus Dei est hic*, here is the finger of God. And in considering this, if you have anything of God in you, it will make you to seek out after this God, and to love this God, and honor this God.

2. I will give you some examples of this occasional, sudden, extemporary meditation of divine things. First, I will give you some examples from Scripture. Prov. 6:6, there the wise man sends the sluggard to the ant, "Go to the ant thou sluggard, consider her ways, and be wise, which having no guide, overseer, or ruler, provideth her meat in the summer." Here you see what a rare meditation a man may have from the little ant, and how the sluggard is sent to behold the ant, to be ashamed of his sluggishness. Let that sight put you in mind of your laziness.

In Jeremiah 8:7, there God sends the unthankful Israelite to the stork, and the turtle, and the crane, and the swallow. "The stork in the heaven knoweth her appointed time, and the turtle and the crane, and the swallow observe the time of their coming." Here you have a sudden and occasional meditation from the creatures of God, the turtle, the crane, the swallow, to observe the time of their coming. The stork at such a time of the year goes out of the land, and at such a time of the year comes into the land; but my people (*there is the meditation*) "know not the judgments of the

Lord." And in this way Christ sends the distrustful Christian to the fowls of the air, and to the lilies of the field, Matt. 6:26, "Behold the fowls of the air for they sow not, neither do they reap nor gather into barns, yet your heavenly father feedeth them, (*here is an occasional meditation*) are you not better than many sparrows? And why take you thought for raiment? consider the lilies of the field how they grow, they toil not, neither do they spin, and yet I say unto you that even Solomon in all his glory was not arrayed like one of these."

You have another example in John 4 where Christ, discoursing with the woman of Samaria, and intreating some water from the woman, takes an occasion from the water of the well to discourse of the water of life. And John 6, from the loaves Christ fed the people with, he takes an occasion to discourse on the bread of life, "You follow me for the loaves," Christ says, "but labour not for the meat that perisheth, but labour for the meat that endureth for ever. I am the bread of life that came down from heaven." Christ takes occasion from the natural bread to meditate on the bread of life, the bread of heaven.

To give you some other examples, I read in St. Augustine, that he had a water-course near his lodging, a great flowing down of waters; and observing how sometimes the water went down silently, and sometimes it made a great noise. From the consideration of the different streams of the water, he made a rare discourse of the *Order of Providence*, the manner how God governs the world in order.

There was a minister, Mr. Deering in Queen Elizabeth's days, a man of famous memory, in whose life it is reported, that just when he was dying, the sun shone on him; and he takes occasion from that most excellently to discourse of that *Sun of Righteousness*, of the glory of heaven, of the happiness he was going to.

I have likewise read, that Mr. Eske, and Dr. Hall (who in his book *of Meditation* quotes this example) were hearing a concert of music, and this holy minister, Mr. Eske, being a very godly man, all of a sudden was so strangely transported with the thoughts of the joys of heaven, that he said with a great deal of passion, "What music, sirs, shall there be in heaven! O the spiritual joy and melody that there we shall have!"

There is a story of two Cardinals in the Council of Constance, that riding abroad for their recreation, they saw a poor countryman weeping, and when they came to him, they asked him, "Why do you weep?" He answers, "Do you see this toad here that lies before me, God might have made me a toad; I am weeping because I never was sufficiently thankful that God did not make me a toad; (you see this poor Country-man takes an occasion from the sight of the toad to raise up his heart in thankfulness to God), and these two Cardinals when they heard him say so, they made use of the speech of St. Augustine, the poor and laboring men get to heaven, and we scholars go down to hell with all our learning. They were ashamed to see what a good use the countryman made of the sight of the toad.

There is another story of a godly old man, that beholding a harlot how curiously she trimmed herself to please her wicked lover, he falls weeping, and being asked, "Why do you weep?" He answers, "I weep to see this lewd woman and what care she takes to dress herself to please her lover, and that I should never take so much care to dress my soul to please my God."

I have read of Ignatius the Martyr, that when he heard the clock strike, he would have this meditation, "Now there is one hour more that I must answer for."

I have read of Fulgentius, that rare scholar, that when he came to heathenish Rome, and saw the Emperor ride in triumph, he broke out into this exclamation, "If there is so much glory in Rome here on earth, O what will be the glory of Heaven!"

I could be infinite in these stories; only I will give you one more, and that is of a heathen-man, Galen, famous for his skill in medicine. When he was viewing the composure of man's body, and beholding its curious workmanship, the story says he fell to sing a hymn to his Creator, "None but a God could make such a body; there must needs be a God that has worked so curiously the members of man's body."

3. Give me leave to give you some *motives* to persuade you to practice this. It is in vain to hear my discourses, unless you endeavor to put them into practice. Now I will give you these motives.

1. This way of meditation may be done at all times; this will not hinder your calling. You that are poor men, and do not have time for solemn meditation during the week-

day, that are laboring men, and cannot spare an hour for solemn and deliberate meditation, you may make use of this sudden, ejaculatory, occasional meditation, even when you are at your day's work. You may make use of your day's work of the things that you are working about, to stir up your hearts to heavenly things; for there is nothing in the world but a good Christian may make a heavenly use of; and therefore, there is no one that can say that he has no leisure for this way of meditation.

2. This is a way of meditation, that a man may practice in all places, and in all companies. A godly man once said to me, "I thank God I can be in heaven when I am in the midst of the crowd in Cheapside; in the midst of the noise I can have a heavenly meditation." There is no place, no company, which can hinder you from this occasional, sudden, ejaculatory meditation.

3. There is nothing easier than this ejaculatory meditation to you that are spiritual; deliberate and solemn meditation is very hard and difficult; but this way of meditation is very easy. The reason is this, because every creature of God is a teacher of some good thing. You cannot behold a spider, but you may make some good use of it. The Scripture makes many rare uses of a spider; a wicked man may be looked on in a spider, as in a glass; and the hope of a wicked man is compared to a spider's web; as a spider puts his trust in his web, and spends a great deal of pains in weaving his web, and when it is woven, it is easily pulled down, there is no stability in it. So, a wicked man puts his trust in his hope of heaven, which is as vain as a spider's web.

And the Scripture tells you how by all the money a wicked man gets by unlawful means, he weaves a spider's web. That is a rare use the prophet Isaiah makes of the spider, which is one of the meanest of all the creatures of God; a spider and a toad, and a viper, even the venomous creatures, a man may make rare use of. Isa. 59:5-6, "They hatch cockatrice eggs, and weave the spider's web: he that eateth of their eggs dieth; and that which is crushed breaketh out into a viper. Their webs shall not become garments, neither shall they cover themselves with their works." That man is a very bad scholar that can spell nothing out of ten hundred thousand books, for every creature is as it were a book to teach us some good thing. Now that man is but a very ill scholar that can make use of none of these books.

4. In this lies the excellency of a Christian, that he is able to spiritualize natural things. In this lies the wickedness of a wicked man, a wicked man naturalizes spiritual things. But in this lies the godliness of a godly man, a godly man spiritualizes natural things. The wicked man carnalizes even spiritual things. When he is at an ordinance, like the sacrament, if he is not truly godly, he carnalizes and naturalizes even that spiritual ordinance of the sacrament. But a godly Christian is like a heavenly scientist, that can draw heaven out of a spider as it were, draw something of God out of a toad. Heavenly instructions out of a toad, out of a viper, out of any creature of God, and even much more out of the heavens, sun, moon and stars. You wonder at the chemist, when he can extract the four elements out of a mixed body. Much more excellent is that Christian which

can extract heaven out of every creature of God, that can heavenlize and spiritualize the creatures of God. And let me tell you a little to amplify this motive.

1. In this a true Christian exceeds the brute beasts; the brute beasts can enjoy the creature, but he cannot reflect on the creature. He enjoys the good things of God, but he cannot behold God in these things, he cannot improve them for God. But now a true Christian makes all these things to be glasses to see God in, pictures to behold God in; the goodness of God, and the wisdom of God; and he endeavors to receive spiritual instruction by them.

2. In this a child of God exceeds all wicked men; there is no wicked man that can use the creatures spiritually. It is above his sphere. A wicked man makes the creatures a wall of separation between God and him, not a glass to see God. There is no wicked man who uses the creatures of God as a mirror to behold God in, or as a footstool to raise him up to God, or a ladder to climb to God by. This is proper only to a godly man.

5. Consider this, it is the greatest affront you can offer to God, not to take spiritual notice of his creatures; not to make a spiritual use of his creatures. God has put mankind on the stage of this world, and God has made all the Creatures for man's use, and God has made man to be the *tongue* to praise him for all his creatures; and if man does not praise him, God loses the praise of all the whole creation. God made all the creatures for man, and man to praise him for all the creatures; which if man neglects, God loses the glory of the whole of creation. How does the sun, and the

moon, and the stars praise God! The prophet David calls on the ice, and the snow, and the rain, and all the creatures of God, to praise God. How do they praise God? How does the fire and the water praise God? When we praise God for these things, then they praise God when we use them for God, and draw heavenly things, spiritual instruction out of them; and when we do not do this, we offer the greatest affront that can be offered to God in that kind, and we deprive God of the glory of the whole Creation.

6. It is a soul-destroying sin not to observe the works of God, and to make a good use of them. Psalm 28:5, "Because they regard not the works of the Lord, nor the operation of his hand, he shall destroy them, and not build them up."

These are the six motives you should heed. Now in a word, to put an end to this part of the discourse, let me beseech and intreat you, that you would put this duty in practice. Let me tell you, sirs, that though occasional, ejaculatory meditation you should be as a *parenthesis* (as one very well says) in your worldly businesses. Yet this parenthesis is more worth than all your worldly business; yes, it signifies more than all your worldly business. As for example, (I will conclude my discourse by giving you a little help). When I rise in a morning; what an excellent thing would it be for a man to meditate of the great morning of the resurrection, and that it shall be as easy for men to rise out of the grave at the great resurrection, as it has been for me this morning to arise out of my bed. And when the sun begins to arise, and we behold the sun shining, what a rare meditation is it to consider there will a day come in which the Sun of Righteousness shall come in the clouds, and all his holy Angels with him, and all the saints at that day shall shine as so many suns in the firmament. O! what a glorious day will that be, when there shall be as many suns as there are saints! There shall be as many suns as there are stars now in a bright shining night in the heaven. And when you are going abroad, it would be very comely, spiritual and useful to remember, that you have two companions always going with you, that is God and the devil, (pardon me that I join them together). You have the judge and your accuser to go with you; wheresoever you walk in the daytime, one devil or other is always waiting on you, and God is always present with you, who will call you to an account for all that you do. The devil scores up all that you do, to accuse you afterward. And when you walk abroad and see a debauched wicked man, it is an excellent thing to have a meditation, and to say, "Blessed be God that has made me to differ from this man; if it had not been for the grace of God, I had been as wicked as this man." And when you meet with a godly man, a man eminent for godliness, O! put up a prayer to God that he would make you as godly; and mourn that you are not as godly as he. When you meet with a learned man, or a wise man, or a beautiful creature, it is a very excellent meditation to consider, if there is so much beauty, so much wisdom in the creature, O! what is there in God, who is the ocean of beauty! If there is so much comeliness, so much excellency here below, O! what is there above! It is a rare thing to use the creatures reflexively; it is idolatry to use the creature terminately; but the admirable, the superlative excellency of a Christian is to use the creature reflexively; to reflect from the creature to the Creator. So likewise, when you are in your shop, and weighing your commodities, would it not be an excellent meditation, to think there will a time come, when God will weigh you in a balance, and weigh your actions, and weigh all that you do! And meditate on that text, Proverbs 11:1, "A false balance is an abomination to the Lord." And so likewise, when you walk in the fields, and behold the grass that grows, and behold the flowers of the field, does it not become you to meditate, that all flesh is grass, and all the glory of the world is but the goodliness of the grass; and all earthly things are but like the beauty of a flower? My little child that I love so much, is but like this flower, it is beautiful, but it is but fading. And when you see a wicked man grow great by wicked ways, would it not be a very comfortable thing to remember that text, "Fret not thy self because of evil doers, neither be thou envious against the workers of iniquity, for they shall be soon cut down as the grass, and wither as the green herb." And you that are merchants, when you are on the exchange, a short sudden ejaculation would not be hurtful, but helpful to you. As for example, to remember that as you are merchant-adventurers for earthly things, so you are all merchant-adventurers for heaven, and your souls are in the midst of the sea of this world; this world is like a sea, and your soul is here like a ship at sea, and is in danger to be split upon the rocks, in danger of pirates, and in danger of being lost. Your ships have not half so many dangers as your souls have; the temptations of the devil, the allurements of the world, the corruptions of your own hearts. Now to consider, as in the exchange, what is become of such and such a ship, so to ask your soul in what case is your soul now, that is on the sea of this world; and then to go to the ensuring-office, (you know you have your ensuring-offices, in which you ensure your ships at sea) to get your souls insured by reconciliation with God; and by true faith, manifested by holiness and righteousness, to get your souls *assured*, that they may come safe to the haven of happiness.

In a clear bright frosty winter-night, when you go out and behold the array of heaven, a multitude of bright stars, what a rare thing were it to meditate. This glorious firmament is but *the stable* as it were, the *out-houses* of that heaven where I am to go; it is but the outward court, the wash-house, as I may say. And if the stable and out-houses are so glorious, O! what is the inward palace! Above the spangled heavens is my Father's house, where I hope to live forever with God, and there my Christ is now interceding for me, and by the power of his Spirit shall I be brought one day to that house. O! when will that time come! when will my soul mount through these heavens into the heaven of heavens! Now is not this comely for a Christian? Will not this *heavenlize* you, and *spiritualize* you? And then when you go to bed at night, to remember, I have one day more to answer for; to remember there will a last night come, after which there will be no day but the resurrection of everyone. Remember your last night, your concluding night, the end of your life.

I have been overly long in this, a great deal more than I thought. I end here to this discourse of occasional meditation.

Chapter 2:
Solemn Meditation

There is a second sort of meditation, and that is which I call set, solemn and deliberate meditation. When a man sets apart an hour a day it may be, sets apart some time, and goes into a private closet, or a private walk, and there solemnly and deliberately meditates on the things of heaven.

Now concerning this meditation, I shall handle by God's assistance these two particulars:

1. I will show you its nature.

2. I will show you its necessity.

1. The nature of this duty, what this meditation is, that I would press you to: I will describe it in two particulars.

1. This holy meditation is a dwelling and abiding on things that are holy; it is not only a knowing of God, and a knowing of Christ, but it is a dwelling on the things we know. As the bee that dwells and abides on the flower, to suck out all the sweetness that is in the flower, so, to meditate on God and Christ, and the sacrament, is to dwell on God, and the sacrament, to suck out all the sweetness we can in the things we meditate on. As we read of Anna in Luke 2:37, "She continued in the Temple praying and fasting day and night." To meditate, is to continue and fix ourselves and our hearts upon the things we know; this meditation in Scripture is called a *holy musing*, as in Psalm 39:3, "My heart was hot within me, while I was musing;" to meditate is to muse, or else it is to commune with our own hearts. Psalm

4:4 says, "Stand in awe and sin not: commune with your own heart upon your bed and be still." It is a communing, a consulting with our own hearts; or if you will, it is a thinking to ourselves. It is expressed in this way in 1 Kings 8:47, "If they shall think to themselves in the land whither they were carried captive, and repent." The Hebrew word there is, *if they shall bring back to their hearts*, or *if they shall reflect upon themselves;* for meditation is a reflecting act of the soul, by which the soul is carried back to itself, and considers all the things that it knows. Meditation is an inward act of the soul, a spiritual act, by which the soul recoils on itself, and looks back on itself, and considers all the things that concern its everlasting happiness; and if I am not mistaken, it is rarely typified under the Law in two ways.

1. By those beasts that chew the cud; you shall read in Leviticus 11 of the clean beasts, and the unclean beasts. Now the clean beasts were such as chew the cud, of those they were to eat. Now, the unclean beasts were those that did not chew the cud. A meditating Christian is one that chews the cud, that chews on the truths of Jesus Christ, that does not only hear good things, but when he has heard them, chews them over, ruminates on them, so that they may be more fit for digestion and concoction, and spiritual improvement. An unclean Christian is one that does not chew the cud, that does not ruminate, and ponder, and think to himself about the things of heaven.

2. Another type of this rare grace of meditation, is that of the beasts in Ezekiel chapter 1. Ezekiel saw beasts

that had eyes within and without, (1:18). Their wings were "full of eyes" round about them. And so likewise, the beasts of Revelation 4:6, "Round about the throne were four beasts full of eyes before and behind." This is a notable and a rare type of meditation; for meditation is nothing else but looking thoroughly into the things of God; a looking before and behind, as I may so speak. A meditating Christian is a man *full of eyes,* that does not only know God, but sees much of God. There is another metaphor to express it in Psalm 119:59, "I thought on my ways, and turned my feet unto thy testimonies." The word in the Hebrew is taken from businessmen, that when they buy a commodity, they turn it over, and over, and over again. They look all about it into every part. Meditation is a thorough contemplation, and a thorough consideration of the things of God; a meditating Christian is full of eyes, full of heavenly understanding.

2. It is an act of the heart as well as of the head; it is not only a speculative knowledge of divine things, but a practical knowledge. It is not only an act of the intellect and understanding, but of the will and affections; it is an affective grace as well as an intellective grace. It is said of the blessed virgin Mary, "she pondered all these sayings in her heart." She did not only think of them with her head, but she pondered on them with her heart. And you shall read in Deut. 4:39, "Know therefore this day, and consider it in thy heart." A true meditation is when a man so meditates on Christ as to get his heart inflamed with the love of Christ. So, meditate on the truths of God to be transformed into

them. Meditate on sin as to get your heart to hate sin. Be musing about God in such a way as to kindle a fire in the whole soul, as David expresses it in Psalm 39:3, "While I was musing, the fire burnt." When a man so contemplates on God, that his heart is all on fire with the love of God, when he so thinks on the sacrament, that his heart is all on fire with a holy thirsting after the sacrament, this is when the heart is affected with the meditation of the head. David says in Psalm 104:34, "My meditation of him shall be sweet." This is true meditation, when we so meditate of God, as to taste a sweetness in God. It is when meditation does not rest in the intellectual part, but flows into the will and affection, that the heart is all inflamed with the things we meditate on. There are many great scholars that meditate much of God, and Christ, and heaven, and yet they are never holier for their meditation; and the reason is, because they meditate on these things merely to find out curious notions of God, and Christ, and heaven. But they do not meditate on these things to get their hearts affected, to get heavenly and divine hearts. Therefore, you shall see many scholars as undevout, and as unholy as other people, though they know more, and meditate more. And I have found it by experience, that there are many poor lay people that get all the more better by meditation than great scholars; the great scholar's meditation many times vanishes into empty speculations, and into notions and opinions. But the honest godly man's meditation is all for practice. He meditates on sin to hate it, of the sacrament to hunger after it, of God to love him, of Christ to be inflamed with a desire after him. And therefore, he increases in getting more good many times by meditation. The butterfly will dwell on the flower as well as the bee, but the butterfly only sucks the flower that she may paint her wings with it. She is not useful to make honey. She does not suck honey from the flower. So, there are many scholars, many men that meditate much on the things of God to paint their wings, that is, to get more knowledge of God and heaven, and more curious expressions of heaven, but it is the honest Christian, the plain-hearted Christian, that meditates on God like the bee, to suck out the sweetness of God. He meditates on Christ to get his heart burning in love to Christ. This is the rare grace of meditation.

Meditation must walk through and enter into three doors, or else it will never do you any good.

1. It must get into the door of the understanding, and there it is seated, there is the proper place of meditation; but if it rests there, you are never better for it.

2. It must get into the door of your heart, and of your affections; and you must never leave meditating until it gets into that door as well.

3. The door of your conversation; for your meditation must not rest in the affections. It must also have influence into your conversation, to make your conversation more holy. You must so meditate on God as to walk as God walks; and so, to meditate on Christ as to prize him, and live in obedience to him. A nurse that has a nurse-child, will cut the meat, and will many times chew the meat for the child, but she will not *eat* the meat, but give it to the child. For, if she should chew the meat and eat it up herself, the child might

starve for all her chewing it, and preparing it. It is this way with the grace of meditation. Meditation, while it is in the understanding, chews on the things of God, and of Christ, and of heaven, but when the understanding has chewed these things, it must not devour all these things itself, but it must convey the meat it has chewed (as the meat is conveyed from the stomach into the liver, and then into the heart, and then into all the other parts of the body) into the heart, and into the will, and into the affections, and into the conversation. This is the first, the admirable nature of this grace.

2. I come to show you its necessity. I do this, rather, that I might provoke you all to its practice; for I am very confident there are *few* people that practice this duty of meditation. There are few that know how to practice it; but there are very few that make a conscience effort to practice it. Even those of you that make a conscience effort to pray twice a day in your family, seldom make conscience once a day of meditation, no, not even once a week. And therefore, that I might awaken myself and you, give me leave to show you the great necessity of practicing the *duty* of meditation.

Chapter 3:
Two Ways of Meditation

For the duty of meditation, I will show its two manner of ways of doing this. 1. By considering the mischief that flows from the lack of practicing this duty. 2. By showing you the advantage and spiritual benefit that you will gain by practicing this duty.

1. I shall show you the woeful inconveniences, and the intolerable mischiefs that come from the lack of practicing this duty of meditation. I will bring them to two heads.

1. I will show you, that the lack of practicing this duty is the cause of all sin.

2. It is the cause of all punishment.

1. I will show you, that the lack of practicing this duty is the cause of all sin: and I will show you instances of this in various particulars.

1). The reason why people harden their hearts in sin, and do not repent of their sins, but go on obstinately, is for a lack of meditation. Jeremiah 8:6, "I hearkened and heard, but they spake not aright, no man repented him of his wickedness, saying, what have I done?" They did not repent, because they did not reflect on what they did; they did not think to themselves, so the phrase is, "If any man bethink himself and repent," (1 Kings 8:47). They did not say, "I am undone by what I have done; I have lost God and heaven by what I have done; and if I do not repent, I am an undone creature forever." No man repented of his wickedness, because no man considered what he had done; for if you consider the evil that is in sin, you dwell and abide on it, you commune with your own hearts, and seriously consider what an evil and bitter thing it is to sin against God. You did not dare to willingly sin against God. But the reason why men go on rashly, heedlessly, obstinately in sin, is for a lack of meditation on the evil of sin.

2). The reason why all the sermons we hear do us no more good, is for a lack of divine meditation. It is with sermons as it is with food. It is not having food on your table which will feed you, but you must eat it; and not only eat it, but concoct it, and digest it, or else your food will do you no good. It is the same way with sermons. It is not hearing sermons which will do you good, but it is the concocting them, digesting them by meditation; the pondering in your hearts what you hear, must do you good. And one sermon well digested, well meditated on, is better than twenty sermons without meditation. As for example, a little food well digested will nourish a man more than a great deal of food if it breeds a sour stomach, if it does not digest; it is the digesting of food that nourishes a man. Now, meditation is that which will digest all the sermons you hear. There are some men sick of a disease, that whatever they eat comes up presently, the food never does them any good. This is the way it is with the custom of many of you. You hear a sermon, you go away, and never think of it afterward; this is just like food that you vomit up. There is a disease that some men have, that all the food they eat goes through them, it never abides with them; now this meat never nourishes. So, it is with the sermons you hear during the week. I am afraid the sermons you hear on the Sabbath-day go through you, you hear them, and that is all you do; but you never seek by meditation to root them in your hearts. That is the reason why you are so lean in grace though you are so fully fed with sermons. It is with sermons as it is with a cast on an arm or leg. If a man has a wound in his body and places a bandage of some kind to the wound, this bandage will never heal him, unless it abides on the wound. If a man takes it away the cast or bandage as soon as it is laid on him, it will never do him any good. It is the same way with sermons. If when you have heard a sermon, you never ponder and meditate on it, it is just like a bandage put on, and then pulled off again. And I am confident the great reason why we have so many lean hunger-starved Christians, that are lean in knowledge, and lean in grace, though they hear sermon after sermon, (it may be on the Sabbath-day they will hear four or five sermons) is because they concoct and digest nothing. They never ponder and meditate on what they hear; and this is that which our Savior Christ speaks about by the seed that was sown by the wayside. This is meant of a man, that hears the word, and never thinks of it after he has heard it but allows the devil to steal it out of his heart. This is like the husbandman that sows the seed in the highway, you know he never plows it, he never looks that that should come to anything. There are many of you where the sermons you hear are like the seed sown in the highway, you never cover it by meditation, you never think of it, after you have heard it. That is the reason you get no more good by what you hear.

3). The reason why the promises of God no more affect your hearts when the saints of God taste no more sweetness in the promises, is because you do not ponder and meditate on them. It is with the promises of the Gospel as it is with a cordial. If a man does not chew his cordial but swallows it down whole, he will never taste any great sweetness, in it. The way to taste the sweetness is to chew it. So, the promises of God are full of heavenly comfort, but you will never enjoy this comfort unless you chew them by meditation. As it is with spices, unless they are bruised, they never smell sweet; and as it is with a pomander, unless you rub it, you will never smell its sweetness. You will not ever taste the heavenly comfort that is in the promises of the Gospel, unless you rub them, unless you bruise them, unless you chew them by meditation. And the reason why the saints of God walk so uncomfortably all their lives long, is because they do not chew these promises.

4). The reason why the threatenings of God make no more impression on our hearts, is for a lack of meditation. There are terrible threatenings against sin in the word, but alas, there are few people affected with these threatenings. The threatenings of God in Scripture are like the rattling of hail on the tiles of the roof, they make a great noise, but they make no impression; and what is the reason? It is for a lack of meditation. We do not lay them to heart, we do not consider that these threatenings belong to us, as long as we continue in our sins. O! if a wicked man would meditate solemnly on the threatenings of God, it would make his heart ache, especially when the spirit of bondage goes along with them.

5). The reason why the mercies of God do no more good on us, is for lack of meditation. There are many mercies that all of us have received from God, many personal mercies, and many family-mercies, and all these mercies are many motives to holy service. Now what is the reason the saints of God bury the mercies of God in forgetfulness, and are not more thankful for mercies? The reason is for lack of meditation, Isaiah 1:2-3, "Hear, oh heavens, and give ear, oh earth, for the Lord hath spoken: I have nourished and brought up children, and they have rebelled against me; the ox knoweth his owner, and the ass his masters crib, but Israel doth not know, my people doth not consider." That is the reason why they are so unthankful. It is with the mercies of God as it is with the fire, if a man walks by the fire and does not sit at it, it will never heat him much. If he is cold, he must abide at the fire, or else he will never be hot. So, it is not a slight thought of the mercies of God that will affect your hearts, but it must be that you dwell on them by meditation, which will warm your hearts. Now because we do not meditate on these mercies, we do not solemnly consider the mercies of God, therefore that is why they do no more good on our hearts. In Psalm 106 we have a psalm set on purpose to demonstrate the unthankfulness of the people of Israel, as it is in verse 3, "We have sinned with our fathers, we have committed iniquity, we have done wickedly; our fathers understood not thy wonders in Egypt, they remembered not the multitude of thy mercies, but provoked him at the sea, even at the Red-sea." What is the reason they were so unthankful? It was because they did not meditate on the mercies of God.

6). The reason why afflictions do not work more on us, and why we are never better for God's afflicting hand, is for lack of meditation. It is a rare text, Eccles. 7:14. "In the day of prosperity be joyful, but in the day of adversity consider." Times of affliction are times of meditation; and what must we consider of in the day of adversity? We must consider who it is that afflicts us, and why we are afflicted, and what we shall do to have our afflictions sanctified. We must consider the meaning of God's rod, and how we may be taught by these afflictions in spiritual things. Now because we do not meditate on God, and on his afflicting hand when we are afflicted, because we have slight heads under our afflictions, therefore, it is that we get no better by our afflictions. I have observed many of us (the Lord pardon it to us) as soon as ever we are recovered from our afflictions, we forget God presently. We never consider the mercies of God in recovering us, and then we return to our old vomit again, for lack of meditation.

7). The reason why the Providences of God make no impression on our hearts, is for lack of this grace of meditation. The providences of God are very mysterious, and God in the government of the world walks in the clouds. And truly I am very confident, that which God especially requires of his children in these days, is to meditate on his providences, as well as on his ordinances. There are many rare lessons to be learned from considering the providences of God; the providence of God toward England, and toward Scotland, and toward the ministry. God is now depriving you of minister upon minister, many ministers the Lord has taken from you. God is, as I may so speak, disburdening the nation of this great burden of the ministry, which is a burden to a great many. God takes his ministers up to heaven. Now what is the reason that the providences of God of late years do no more good, though they have been wonderful toward England, Scotland, and Ireland, towards all sorts of people? The reason why we are never bettered by them, is because we do not study the meaning of all these providences. Isa. 57:1, "The righteous perisheth, and no man layeth it to heart, and merciful men are taken away, none considering that the righteous is taken away from the evil to come." This is the reason why we do not get any more good by the death of the godly, and by the providences of God, because we do not lay them to heart; we do not muse and study on them.

8). What is the reason that the saints of God are so distrustful of God's providences, when they are ready presently to sink, and to say they are undone? It is for a lack of meditation. Therefore, Christ, Luke 12 says, "Take no thought what you shall eat, or what you shall put on; consider the ravens, for they neither sow nor reap, which neither have store-house nor barn, and God feedeth them; how much more are ye better than the fowls? Consider the lilies how they grow, they toil not, they spin not; and yet I say unto you, that Solomon in all his glory was not arrayed like one of these." Did you consider the lilies, and the ravens, did you study the love of God to you, you would not distrust him under any sad Providences? The reason why the Saints of God are so full of unbelief, when they are in a low condition, is for lack of meditation; they do not consider the ravens, and the lilies, they do not study the promises that God has made to his children in their lowest condition.

9). The reason why the professors of religion are so censorious of other men, and so little censorious of themselves, why they judge every man, and examine every man but themselves, (which is the condition of these days) it is for a lack of meditation. Matthew 7, "Judge not that ye be not judged: for with what judgment ye judge, ye shall be judged: and with what measure you mete, it shall be measured to you again. And why beholdest thou the mote that is in thy brothers eye, but considerest not the beam that is in thy own eye?" If men reflected more on themselves, they would censure themselves more, and others less. And the reason why people are so rash in censuring, is for a lack of self-reflection.

10). The reason why professors of religion offer the sacrifices of fools to God, when they come to worship him; why they pray headily and rashly, why they rush on ordinances without preparation, is for lack of meditation. Eccl. 5:1, "Keep thy foot when thou goest to the house of God and be more ready to hear than to offer the sacrifices of fools, for they consider not that they do evil. Be not rash with thy mouth and let not thy heart be hasty to utter anything before God." Why do people rush on the sacraments without preparation, rush on sermons, rush on prayer, rush on holy duties? It is because they do not consider what they do.

11). What is the reason that people do not prepare any further for death? Because they do not consider the shortness of life. They do not meditate of the vanity of this life, of the certainty and uncertainty of death; and therefore, it is said in Deut. 32:29, "Oh that they were wise, that they understood this, that they would consider their latter end!" Because men do not consider their *latter end*, therefore it is that they are so unprepared for their latter end.

12). And lastly, what is the reason that we come so unworthily to the sacrament? And when we are there, we gaze up and down, and carry ourselves so unseemly at that ordinance? What is the reason that we lose all the fruit of that ordinance, but merely for a lack of preparation before we come, and meditation when we have come? Now preparation cannot be without meditation; preparation includes meditation in it.

2. The lack of the practice of this duty is the cause of all punishment. Isa. 12:11, "The whole land is laid desolate, because no man layeth it to heart." O! this is the cause of the sword that has drunk so much blood in this nation, no man lays to heart the judgments of the Lord, therefore the land is become desolate. Psalm 28:5, "Because they regard not the works of the Lord, nor the operation of his hand, he shall destroy them, and not build them up." Because they do not meditate on God's works, therefore, the Lord will destroy them. Let me add that which is even above all this, for God to give a man over to a slight spirit, an "unmeditating" spirit,

to a rashness and slightness of spirit. This is one of the *greatest* judgments in the world. A man of a slight head can never have a good heart; a slight hearted Christian can never be a good Christian. He that thinks slightly of God, will speak slightly of God. He that speaks slightly of God, will worship God slightly. He that slights God, God will slight him. There cannot be a more cursed frame of spirit, than to be given over to an inconsiderate frame of spirit; an inconsiderate Christian is an inconsiderable Christian. Isa. 42:24-25, "Who gave Jacob for a spoil, and Israel to the robbers? did not the Lord, he, against whom we have sinned? for they would not walk in his ways, neither were they obedient to his law. Therefore, he hath poured upon him the fury of his anger, and the strength of battle, and it hath set him on fire round about, yet he knew not; and it burned him, yet he laid it not to heart." Here is the curse of curses, not so much to be burnt, as not to know it; not so much to have the wrath of God on us, but to not lay it to heart. This is a sign of the greatest fury of God, for a man to be given over to slightness of spirit when he is under the judgments of God, and so he does not regard or lay them to heart.

And in this way I have been somewhat long in setting out to you the mischiefs that flow from the lack of practicing the grace of meditation; and I do this to provoke you all to be humbled before God for not practicing this duty, (for I am confident your consciences will tell you that you do not practice it) and to convince you of the necessity of the practicing of this duty, which is quite dead and buried in the world.

Chapter 4:
Benefits of Divine Meditation

That I may be God's instrument to stir you up to a conscientious practice of this duty of heavenly meditation, I shall show you (secondly) its necessity from the benefits and advantages that will come to Christians by a conscientious practice of the duty. I will show you this in three particulars.

1. It is a mighty help to working and procuring all grace.

2. It is a mighty help to preserve and increase grace.

3. It is a mighty help to arm us against the devil and all his temptations.

1. Meditation, when it is sanctified, is a mighty help to begetting all grace. This I will show in diverse particulars.

1). It is a mighty help to work in us repentance and reformation of life. David says in Psalm 119:59, "I thought on my ways, and turned my feet unto thy testimonies." I thought on my ways, that is, I considered the evil of my ways, and what a bitter thing it is to sin against God. What a dishonor I have brought on God by my evil ways, and what a scandal I have brought on religion. Ezek. 36:31, "Then shall you remember your own evil ways, and your doings that were not good, and shall loath yourselves in your own sight for your iniquities, and for your abominations." A conscientious meditation of the evil of sin is a divine hammer to break your hearts for sin, and from sin; for if you consider the Majesty of God that is offended by the least sin, if you consider the infinite wrath of God against sin, if you consider the affronts that are offered to God by sin, that every sin is a dethroning of God, a robbing of God, a striking through the name of God, if you consider the pollution that is in sin, that sin makes you like the devil, if you further consider the mischief that sin brings on us, this would be a hearty remedy against such things. Sin deprives you of the beatifical vision. It shuts you out of heaven. It binds you over to everlasting burnings.

Again, have you considered the patience of God, and the goodness of God towards you yet, notwithstanding all your sins, and what an unkind thing it is to sin against so good a God? And have you further considered what Christ has done to purchase pardon for your sins, and how Christ has shed his blood for such wicked wretches as you are? If you have sanctifyingly meditated on these things, it would mightily provoke you to repent of your sins, and to turn to God. And therefore, you shall read concerning Peter, after he had denied Christ in Mark 14:72, "The cock crew, and Peter called to mind the word Jesus said unto him, Before the cock crow twice thou shalt deny me thrice; and when he thought thereon he wept." The meaning of the Greek word is, when he weighed the speech of Christ; when he thought what an unkind thing it was to deny his dear Lord and Master. What happened? This made him weep. If he had not meditated on the evil that he had committed, he would have never wept. And what made the prodigal son return home to his father? You shall see the reason in Luke 15:17, "And when he came to himself, he said, How many hired servants of my father have bread enough, and to spare, and I perish with hunger!" When he came to consider within himself, the misery that he had brought on himself, and that there were many servants in his father's house that had bread enough, "I will arise" he says, "and go to my father, and I will say, Father, I have sinned against heaven," (all this was his meditation and thought in this way in his heart to do this) and he arose and came to his Father."

2. Divine meditation is a mighty help to produce in us a love to God; for as it is with a picture, that has a curtain drawn over it, though the picture is never so beautiful, you cannot see its beauty until the curtain is drawn aside. To an *unconsiderating*, an *unmeditating* Christian, God is as a picture with a curtain drawn over it, he cannot see the beauty of God. Meditation draws the curtain and lets us in to behold all the beauty that is in God; and he that beholds the beauty of God, cannot but love God. As it is said of Socrates, he was so good a man that all that knew him loved him; and if any man did not love him, it was because they did not know him. Much more may I say of God, all that meditate in, and study God, cannot but love him. And the reason why you do not love him, is because you do not study and meditate on God. As it is said in 1 John 4:8, "He that loveth not, knoweth not God, for God is love: he that knoweth God, loveth God." What is the reason the saints in heaven love God so perfectly? Because they always behold his face, they see him, they think on him. And did you meditate on the excellency of God, that God is altogether lovely, that all excellencies are after an infinite manner

centered in God, that there is nothing lovely in the creature, but it is to be found infinitely in the Creator? Did you further consider all the good things that God has done for you; all the blessings and mercies that you have received from God? Did you not only think, but did you *dwell* on these thoughts? If you sit at this fire, it would kindle a mighty flame of divine love in your souls. Therefore, David says in Psalm 39:3, "My heart was hot within me; while I was musing the fire burned." Psalm 104:34, "My meditation of him shall be sweet." If you meditate much on God, you would taste a sweetness in God, that would be as a compass to draw your hearts to the love of God.

3. Divine meditation is a mighty help to work in us a fear of God, for the fear of God is the beginning of wisdom. Now, have you studied the majesty of God, that God has all men, all the devils in a chain, and that only God can hurt us, and that no man can hurt us without God giving him leave? Have you studied the omnipotence of God? If you have, you would fear God, and fear him only. As Isaiah 51:12-13 says, "I, even I am he that comforteth you: who art thou that thou shouldest be afraid of a man that shall die, and the son of man that shall be made as grass, and forgettest the Lord thy maker, that hath stretched forth the heavens, and laid the foundations of the earth!" This is as if he should say, if you remembered and thought on the Lord your God, who made the heavens and the earth, and has all things in his hand, you would not fear a man that dies, *etc.* in Jer. 10:6-7, first the prophet breaks out into an admiration of God, "Forasmuch as there is none like unto thee, O Lord: you are great, and thy

name is great in might: who would not fear thee, O King of Nations? for to thee doth it appertain: forasmuch as among all the wise men of the Nations, and in all their Kingdoms, there is none like unto thee." The meditation of God stirs up the prophet to fear God. Jeremiah 5:22, "Fear ye not me, saith the Lord? will you not tremble at my presence, which hath placed the sand for the bound of the sea, by a perpetual decree that it cannot pass, though the waves thereof toss themselves, yet can they not prevail: though they roar, yet cannot they pass over it." If we meditate on the power of God, we would fear him, and stand in awe of him.

4. This divine meditation is a mighty help to work in us a love to Jesus Christ. Jesus Christ is a fountain sealed, a spring shut up, a garden enclosed. Now you know no man is bettered by owning a book that is sealed up, or a treasure locked up. To a careless Christian, Christ is a fountain sealed, a treasure locked up; but meditation is the key that unlocks the treasury of all the excellencies of Christ and opens the book to let us read all the excellencies that are in him. Meditation, as it were, opens the fountain; and if we studied what Christ is, that he is the choicest of ten thousand, altogether excellent, the brightness of his Father's glory, and the express image of his Person; and if we studied the love of Christ to poor sinners, the height, the depth, the length, the breadth of the love of God toward us; if we studied how Christ became poor to make us rich, how he became a curse to free us from the curse; how he was made sin that we might be made the righteousness of God through him; if we bury ourselves in this meditation, if you take half

an hour in a day to meditate on the excellency of Christ, if you, when you walk in the fields, meditate on the love of Christ, I am confident it would work in you a love to Christ.

5. Divine meditation is a mighty help to enable us to believe and trust in God. To trust:

1. In his providence in all outward straights.

2. In his promises in all spiritual troubles.

1. It will help you to trust in his providence when you are in any straights. When all earthly helps fail, and you are ready to sink, then meditation will raise your faith, and help you to trust in God's providence for his outward provision. Matthew 6:25, "I say unto you (Christ says) take no thought for your life what you shall eat, or what ye shall drink, nor yet for your body what you shall put on; be not solicitous for your outward provision." But how does Christ argue this? What way should we take, that we may not distrust God? He says, meditate on the fowls of the air, "behold the fowls of the air for they sow not, (verse 28). "Why take you thought for raiment, consider the lilies of the field how they grow, they toil not, neither do they spin, and yet I say unto you, that even Solomon in all his glory was not arrayed like one of these." The meditation of the lilies and the fowls of the air is a means to help us to trust in the Lord in the day of our straights.

2. It will enable you to rely on the promises for the good of your souls. If you read the promises of the Bible, and chew them, how sweet would they be. The reason why the promises are not sweet to you, is because you read them, but you do not chew them by meditating on them. If you

meditated on them, they would be sweeter than the honey, and the honeycomb, especially if you joined application with meditation. Abraham was the father of the faithful, and he was strong in faith; and what made him strong in faith? He did not consider his own body now dead, neither the deadness of Sarah's womb, but he considered the promise of God, (Rom. 4:19). And the reason why the saints of God are so void of comfort, and hang their heads down, and walk so disconsolately, is because they consider the deadness of their own souls. They consider their imperfections, but they do not meditate on the promises, their freeness and riches. Matthew 16:8, "Which when Jesus perceived, he said to them, Oh ye of little faith, why reason ye among yourselves, because you have brought no bread?" Here Christ reproves them for a lack of faith; but how did they come to lack faith? "Do you not understand, neither remember the five loaves of the five thousand, and how many baskets ye took up? and do ye not remember the seven loaves of the four thousand, and how many baskets you took up?" This is as if Christ should have said, if you had meditated on my former miracles, you would never have doubted this miracle; but because you do not remember what I have formerly done, therefore that is why you are so full of unbelief. So, the way to fill your souls with comfort is to meditate upon the promises of God.

6. Divine meditation is a mighty help to work in us a contempt of the world, and all worldly things; for the world is like gilded copper. It is an easy matter for a man to mistake gilded copper for true gold, unless he considers what he

takes; for if a man takes gold without consideration, he may quickly be deceived. There is a glittering excellency in the world, its wealth and riches are glorious things to a carnal eye, but meditation of the world will wash away all the paint that is on the world. Studying the vanity of the world, the nothingness of all earthly things, their unsatisfiableness, and their perishing nature, this will take away the glittering excellency that seems to be in the world. And certainly, you would never be so covetous, and so worldly, and desire so much of the world if you meditate on its vanity, as you should do. This is the course Solomon takes. The book of Ecclesiastes is called, "The Book of the Preacher," and its subject is to wean us from the love of the world. But what course does Solomon take? Eccles. 1:3, "I gave my heart to seek and search out by wisdom concerning all things done under heaven." His course was to consider all the creatures that were under the heaven. "I have seen," he says, "all the works that are done under the sun and behold all is but vanity and vexation of spirit." After he had meditated on the world, he goes over the riches and the pleasures of the world, and when he had reckoned them all, he concludes in chapter 2:11, "Then I looked on all the works my hand had wrought, and on the labour that I had laboured to do, and behold all was vanity and vexation of spirit." This is as if he said, I gathered silver and gold, and the peculiar treasure of kings, and of the provinces; I got men-singers, and women-singers, and the delights of the sons of men, as musical instruments, and that of all sorts; so I was great, and increased more than all before me in Jerusalem. Also, my wisdom remained with me, and whatever my eyes desired I kept nothing from them. And when he had looked upon all these glorious excellencies, what was his conclusion? "Behold," he says, "all was vanity and vexation of spirit, and there was no profit under the sun." If we meditate greatly on the vanity of the world, we would not idolize it so much.

7. Divine meditation is a mighty help to work in us the grace of thankfulness for the mercies and blessings we receive from God. Certainly, it is a great duty that lies on us to be thankful for God's mercies. There is no way to stir you up to thankfulness so much as meditation on the mercies of God. He that forgets the mercies of God, cannot be thankful for them. Make note of the course that David takes in Psalm 8:3, "When I consider the heavens, the work of thy fingers, the moon, the stars, which thou hast ordained; then he cries out, "What is man that you are mindful of him! or the son of man that thou visitest him! for thou hast made him a little lower than the angels." When he considered what God had done for man, then he admires the love of God to man, and breaks out into thankfulness. Certainly, a Christian who is forgetful of God's mercies can never be thankful for them; and the way to work thankfulness is to meditate on what God has done for us.

8. Divine meditation is a mighty help to birth in you a preferring of God's house before your own house. It is the great sin of this age in which we live, that every man studies to build his own house, and no man cares for the house of the Lord. We may truly say as Jeremiah says, ""This is Zion, whom no man seeketh after," (Jer. 30:17). Every man seeks

his own interest, and no man cares what becomes of religion. There is a strange kind of lukewarmness that is on the spirits of all men in this age, that men may grow great in themselves, and they do not care what becomes of the House of God. Now divine meditation would make you prefer the building of God's House before the building of your own house. And for this purpose, let me implore you to read Haggai 1:4, "Is it time for you, O ye, to dwell in your cieled houses, and this house lie waste?" It was the sin of the people of Israel that they neglected the building of God's house, and every man strove to grow rich in his own particular way. Now, therefore, "thus saith the Lord of hosts, consider your ways, (here the Prophet calls them to consider) ye have sown much, but bring in little; ye eat, but you have not enough; ye drink but ye are not filled with drink; ye clothe you, but there is none warm. And he that earneth wages, earneth wages to put it into a bag with holes." What was the matter? Because they did not build God's house, therefore, God did not build their house. Verse 7 says, "Thus saith the Lord of Hosts, consider your ways: ye looked for much, but lo it came to little, and when you brought it home, I did blow upon it." Why does the Lord say this? "Because of my house that is waste, and ye run every man into his own house, therefore the heaven over you is stayed from dew, and the earth is stayed from her fruit." God will never settle England, or any country, God will never settle your houses, until you make a conscience effort to build God's house, and until you have more zeal for the house of God than for your own houses. Though you may dream of peace and plenty, yet certainly the Lord will never build your houses, until you build God's house. And therefore, he says further in Haggai 2:17, "I smote you with blasting and with mildew, and with hail in all the labors of your hands, yet ye turned not to me, saith the Lord. Consider now from this day and upward, from the four and twentieth day of the ninth month, even from the day that the foundation of the Lords Temple was laid; consider it, from this day will I bless you." And certainly, the world is greatly mistaken; the way to build your own house, is to join together to settle religion. God will never prosper you, until God's house is settled. And did you meditate on these two chapters, the first and second chapter of Haggai, it would by God's grace work in you a mighty zeal toward settling of the house of God, and to prefer that before settling your own house.

9. Divine meditation will beget in us the desire to keep all the commandments of God. There is no commandment of God but divine meditation when it is sanctified, (I do not say otherwise) will work in us and enable us to keep his word. Deut. 4:39-40, "Know therefore this day, and consider it in thy heart, that the Lord is God in heaven above, and upon the earth beneath there is none else; thou shalt keep therefore his statutes, and his commandments." David says in Psalm 119:55, "I have remembered thy name, Oh Lord, in the night, and have kept thy Law."

2. Divine Meditation is not only a means to beget grace, but it is a mighty help to preserve and increase grace. As the wood preserves the fire; as the oil preserves the flame;

as the water preserves the fish, so meditation preserves your graces. It preserves every grace, and it increases every grace, for meditation is a divine pair of bellows to blow up the sparks of grace. When there is a little fire, meditation will kindle this fire more, and increase it. When you find your love of God grows cold, meditate on the love of God, and this will kindle the love of God in your hearts. When you find the fear of God to diminish in you, meditate on the power of God, that your breath is in his hand, that he has you in his hand. This will increase the fear of God; and when the love of the world increases on you, meditate on its vanity and nothingness, and this will decrease the love of the world.

3. Divine Meditation, as it is a means to work grace, and to increase grace, so it is a mighty means to arm and defend us against all the temptations of the devil, and against all his fiery darts. It is armor of proof against the devil and all his temptations. What made Moses refuse the pleasure, treasures and honors of Egypt? Moses, when he was of age, a young man, and fit to enjoy the pleasures of Egypt, he chose rather to suffer affliction than to enjoy the pleasures of sin. He refused to be called the son of Pharaoh's daughter. What made him do all this? Because he had respect to the recompense of reward, and he beheld him that was invisible. He meditated on the reward he should have in heaven. He knew the pleasures of heaven were better than the pleasures of Pharaoh's court, and he knew the treasures he should have in heaven were better than the treasures he should have in Egypt. Therefore, he chose rather to suffer affliction with the people of God, than to enjoy the pleasures

of sin for a season. He knew he could not enjoy both, and he had an eye to the recompense of reward, he saw him that was invisible; and this made him do all this. He could never have done this without this divine grace of meditation.

What made Joseph refuse to lie with his mistress, when he might have been preferred by lying with her, and had secrecy and security? Why he meditated, "How can I do this and sin against God?" He thought of God, and he would not do it; it was meditation that made him refuse it.

What made the saints of old receive joyfully the spoiling of their goods? Heb. 10:34, "They took joyfully the spoiling of their goods, knowing in themselves that they had in heaven a better and an enduring substance." Because they knew, that is, they considered that they had in heaven an enduring substance, an eternal reward, they should have better riches there; they considered that, and that made them lose their outward estates; they looked for a better estate in Heaven. Bishop Hooper, when he was going to Martyrdom, overnight he discoursed and reasoned with himself. He says, "When I think of the fire, I begin to be afraid, for I fear that fire will burn. But when I think of the fire of hell, the fear of eternal fire makes me willing to endure a temporary fire." He says again, "When I think of the loss of life, I begin to be afraid; I know life is precious; and when I meditate upon these outward enjoyments, outward preferments, I seem unwilling to be burnt; but when I meditate of the joys of heaven, and the preferments that I shall have there, this makes me willing to go through fire, to go through martyrdom to heaven." It was meditation of heaven, and the joys of heaven that made the martyrs come so willingly to the stake and embrace it as a bride does her bridegroom.

Chapter 5:
Application of the Doctrine

I have showed you the great necessity of this grace of meditation. It remains now that I should come to the application of this doctrine.

If this duty of divine meditation is such a necessary duty, as you have heard, then it reproves those Christians that are utterly unaccustomed, and unacquainted with this duty. They are those that receive mercies from God, but are never better for the mercies they receive, because they lack meditation. They do not say in their hearts, "let us fear that God that doth give us the former and the latter rain, as it is," (Jer. 5:23). It reproves those that are guilty of many sins, but do not repent for a lack of consideration, because they do not say in their hearts *what have I done?* It reproves those that meet with many losses and crosses in the world, but are never better for their afflictions, because they do not consider what is the meaning of God's rod, and how they may get their afflictions sanctified; that read the blessed promises of the Gospel, but do not taste the sweetness of them because they do not meditate. They do not see it because they do not meditate or chew on these things. In a word, these are those people that hear many sermons, but are never the better for the sermons they hear, and all because they lack this divine meditation.

The mercies of God, and the promises of God, and the afflictions of God, and the sermons we hear, are like a sovereign bandage, which though it is fit rightly for the wound, if it is taken off the wound as soon as ever it is laid on it, it will never help cure the wound. It is the *abiding* of the bandage on the wound that help cures it. So, it is dwelling on the mercies we receive, chewing on the promises, meditating on the sermons we hear, that will do us good. That man that hears a sermon and forgets it as soon as he has heard it, will get nothing good by it. It is with sermons and mercies as it is with food. A man may eat his meat and never be more nourished if he does not digest it. If he vomits it up as soon as he has eaten it, or if his food presently goes through him, it will do him no good. It is digesting, concocting of food that nourishes a man. So, there are thousands of people that hear sermon upon sermon, and yet are never more holy by what they hear, for lack of digesting the sermons they hear by divine meditation. Now this lack of meditation is a sin, that I persuade myself that most Christians are guilty of. A person cannot exclude themselves from this duty. There are few Christians that are convinced of the necessity of this duty of divine meditation, few that practice this duty. The great God has exercised this English Nation with a variety of providences for many years. We have been these eleven or twelve years in the fire of affliction; we have met with unexpected changes and alterations, but where is the man that lays to heart the providences of God? Where is the man that studies what God is doing with this Nation? And where is he who uses these providences of God to be further sanctified? We may say of most of the nation, as it is in Jer. 12:11, "The whole land is made desolate, because no man layeth it to heart." There is no man that considers what the meaning of God's providences are, the variety and strangeness, and wonderfulness of them. We are like those in Isa. 42:24-25, "Who gave Israel to the spoil, and Israel to the robbers? did not the Lord, he against whom we have sinned? for they would not walk in his ways, neither were they obedient to his law, therefore he hath poured upon him the fury of his anger, and the strength of battle, and it hath set him on fire round about, yet he knew not; and it burned him, but he laid it not to heart." We have been burning, and burning, and consuming, but no man lays it to heart; this is the great sin of this nation; may the Lord humble us. There are four sorts of Christians that are here to be reproved for the lack of the grace of divine meditation.

1. The ignorant Christian, that does not know how to set about the work of meditation for a lack of matter and substance to meditate on; for meditation supposes knowledge. Meditation is a dwelling on that which we know; and therefore, the ignorant Christian cannot be a meditating Christian. He that is ignorant of God cannot meditate of God; he that is ignorant of Christ crucified, cannot meditate of Christ crucified; and this is one reason why so many saints of God are so barren in sacramental meditation, because they know so little of Christ crucified. The ignorance of God and Christ is not only a sin, but it is the root of all sin. It is said in 1 Sam. 2:12 of the two sons of old Eli, "They were sons of Belial, and they knew not the Lord." All sin is wrapped up in ignorance, as a child in swaddling clothes; as toads and serpents grow in dirty and

dark cellars, so all sin grows where ignorance dwells. And therefore, Chrysostom says, "That ignorance is a deep hell." And one says very well, "An ignorant Christian is the devil's shop, in which he forges all manner of wickedness."

2. There is the forgetful Christian: for meditation is a meditating of what we know concerning God and heaven, and the day of judgment. It is a bringing of the things we know, to ourselves, and therefore, a forgetful Christian cannot be a meditating Christian. He that forgets the mercies of God, can never meditate on the mercies of God. This sin of forgetfulness of God is a sin that the children of Israel were very guilty of, (Psalm 106:7). The Prophet complains of them, "our fathers understood not thy wonders in Egypt, they remembered not the multitude of thy mercies, but provoked him at the sea, even at the Red Sea," verse 13, "they soon forgot his works," verse 31, "They forgot God their Saviour, which had done great things in Egypt; therefore he said, that he would destroy them." Forgetting God, and the mercies of God, is the root of all sin, as well as the ignorance of God. Judges 3:7, "The children of Israel did evil in the sight of the Lord, and forgot the Lord their God, therefore they did evil in the sight of the Lord." And therefore, God lays a charge on the children of Israel, that when they came into the land of Canaan, and should have the fulness of all outward blessings, Deut. 8:11, "Beware (*he says*) that thou forget not the Lord thy God, in not keeping his commandments, and his judgments, and his statutes, which I command thee this day: lest when thou hast eaten, and art full, and hast built goodly houses, and dwelt

therein." Verse 14, "Then thy heart be lifted up, and thou forget the Lord thy God." You that forget the mercies of God, God will forget to be merciful to you; and you that do not remember what good things God has done for you, God will in turn take order that you shall have no good things to remember. The saved thief on the cross, when he was dying, his great request to Christ was, "Lord remember me when thou comest into thy Kingdom." It is the great desire of all saints that God would remember them in mercy; but certainly, you that forget the mercies of God, God will forget to be merciful to you.

3. I am to reprove the rash-headed Christian, that rushes on duties, and on ordinances, and public offices, without consideration. They come rashly to the sacrament and kneel down rashly to his private and public devotion. He does not consider before-hand when he comes to worship the Lord our God; this I call the rash-headed Christian, we have many such among us.

And there are four things worthy your observing, that may be said of a rash-headed Christian.

He is a spiritual fool, and all the sacraments he receives, and the prayers he makes, they are the sacrifices of fools, as you have it excellently set down in Eccl. 5:1-2, "Keep thy foot when thou goest to the house of God, and be more ready to hear than to give the sacrifices of fools, for they consider not that they do evil. Be not rash with thy mouth and let not thy heart be hasty to utter anything before God, for God is in heaven, and thou upon earth, therefore let thy words be few." Out of which two verses I gather these two things.

1). That it is the duty of all Christians in all their addresses to God to consider who this God is to whom they draw near; to consider their own vileness, and God's excellency; to consider that God is in heaven and they are on earth.

2). That whoever rushes on ordinances without consideration, he offers up the sacrifice of fools, because he does not consider that he does evil. When you come rashly to public duties here on the Sabbath-day, and you come rashly to the sacrament, and when you are hasty to utter words to God, you come as so many spiritual fools.

2. A rash-headed Christian will many times speak that which he will wish he had not spoken; and he will do that which he shall have cause to repent of. We have many examples of the Saints of God, that have paid dearly for their rash-speaking, and their rash-practicing; for this rashness is a sin that the saints of God are very much subject to. We read of Peter, that he fell three times into this sin in Matthew 16:22. There Christ told Peter, that he must be crucified, and Peter began to rebuke him, saying, "Be it far from thee, Lord, this shall not be unto thee." Peter spoke very rashly. Now Christ said unto him, "Get thee behind me, Satan, you are an offence unto me." And Luke 9, when Christ was transfigured, then Peter began to utter a rash speech, where Peter says to Christ, "Master, it is good for us to be here; and let us make three tabernacles, one for thee, and one for Moses, and one for Elias; not knowing what he said." It

was a rash speech. And then consider especially Luke 22, when Christ told him that one of you shall betray me. He says very rashly, "Master, though all betray thee, yet will not I betray thee." But he spoke rashly, not knowing the deceitfulness of his own heart. We read of the two brethren, James and John, that they spoke very rashly to Christ in Luke 9:54, "When his two disciples James and John saw this, they said, Lord, wilt thou that we command fire to come down from heaven and consume them, even as Elias did? but he turned and rebuked them, and said, Ye know not what manner of spirit ye are of." We read of Moses, that he spoke unadvisedly with his lips, and God was angry with him in Numbers 20. "Shall we bring water for you out of the rock?" He spoke unadvisedly, and the Lord was angry with him. Jephtha made a rash vow, "Whatsoever I see, I will offer in sacrifice." He had cause to repent of that vow. And that which I say of words, I may say of deeds. The saints of God have done many things in their haste, that they have cause to repent of. David rashly gave away the land of innocent Mephibosheth to his servant in 2 Sam. 16:4. Ziba came with a false accusation against his Master, and David rashly without examining the cause, said, "Thine are all that pertained unto Mephibosheth," which was a very sinful and an unjust rash action of David. He gave away all the estate of the master to a cunning servant. And when he came marching against Nabal, he spoke rashly, and was acting rashly. "As the Lord lives," he says, "I will not leave one alive of the house of Nabal." And he came with his army thinking to destroy everyone, if Abigail had not prevented him.

3. A rash-headed Christian will quickly run into error, and into by-paths. As a man that runs hastily is very prone to stumble, so those Christians that rush on the profession of religion, and rush on public offices and ordinances, they are likely to miscarry in them, and they are apt to run into error. For a rash-headed Christian is led more by passion than judgment; he is led more by affection than by reason. He is like a horse without a bridle, like a house without walls, a city without gates. A city without walls and doors is easily robbed. So, a rash-headed Christian is easily comforted by the truths of Christ.

4. A rash-headed Christian will never persevere and hold out to the end. He that takes a profession of religion on him rashly and does not consider before-hand what it will cost him, when this man meets with more difficulty than he is aware of, he will apostatize and fall away. And therefore, it is the speech of our Savior in Luke 14:28, "Which of you intending to build a tower, sitteth not down first, and counteth the cost whether he hath sufficient to finish it? What King going to make war against another King, sitteth not down first and counteth whether he be able with ten thousand to meet him that cometh against him with twenty thousand." Do not let this be offensive to tell you this, and do not let your hearts rise against it. There are many of in this City that took up the Presbyterian persuasion, but they never considered what they took. They took it as an opinion preached and offered up, but as soon as ever they found opposition, they fell from it, because they never considered what it was when they took it. Few men consider seriously

what religion is, and what it is to be a real saint, and a real professor of religion; and therefore, as soon as ever persecution and trouble arise, they fall away for lack of meditation and consideration.

4. I am to reprove especially your slight-headed Christians, that cannot dwell long upon any thing that is good, that rove and wander from one thing to another; this frame of spirit, if I am not mistaken, is *quite opposite* to religion. Do not think I am censorious, for I must profess, I have been long of this opinion, that a slight-headed Christian cannot be a good Christian. Religion is a serious and solemn matter, it is a business of eternity; and I read of religious people in Scripture, that they are commended for their seriousness. It is said of the Virgin Mary in Luke 2:19, "All that heard it wondered at the things that were told them, but she kept all these things and pondered them in her heart." A religious Christian is a thoughtful pondering Christian. Luke 1:66, "All they that heard them, laid them up in their hearts, saying, What manner of child shall this be!" A true saint of God is a considering, thoughtful, serious Christian; therefore a slight-headed Christian is but a slight Christian; for he that thinks slightly of God, will serve him slightly, and speak slightly of him; a slight head produces a slight heart, and a slight life. If the thought of God and Christ make but slight impressions on your soul, your expressions of God and Christ will be more slight. He that thinks slightly of God, God will slight him. A slight-headed Christian is but a vain Christian, and all his religion is but vanity, but like a slight garment, or a slight house that any

wind blows down. The Lord gives you all this to think about it. Most Christians in the world are slight-headed Christians, that think slightly of sin, of God, of Christ, of the day of Judgment. Yes, but you will say to me, "Are all men that have slight heads, hypocrites?"

Answer. I will give you a distinction, that I may not be misunderstood. There is a double slightness of head, there is a slightness of head that is a natural disease, when a man through the weakness of his head cannot dwell long upon anything, when he cannot think of worldly business long, his head will not bear it; now you may be a true child of God and have a weak head, that is not able to think long of anything at all. And there is a slightness of head that is a sinful slightness, and that is, when a man can be serious on the things of the world, can dwell upon worldly businesses, but cannot dwell long upon the things of heaven, cannot be serious about the things of his soul. As soon as ever he comes to prayer, he is slight. As soon as ever he comes to the sacrament, or any holy duty, then he has slight thoughts of God, and of heaven. Such a person was Gallio in Acts 18. When he saw it was a matter of religion, he did not care for any of these things. He says, "if it were a matter of civil right, I would regard it; but seeing it is matter of religion, look ye to it." And Pilate was a slight-headed man, John 18:38, "Pilate saith unto him, what is truth?" that was a good question; and when he had said this, he went out again to the Jews; he never looked for an answer. He had a slight thought that came into his mind that was good, but he went away, and never came and desired Christ to give him answer. I implore you to consider it. A slight-headed Christian can never be a good Christian. If the things of God do not make impression on your hearts, you will never be serious about the things of eternity. These are the four sorts of Christians that are to be reproved for lack of meditation.

But I have another use of reproof. If those are to be reproved that neglect this divine duty of meditation, much more are those to be reproved that meditate on things that are wicked, instead of meditating on the things of heaven. Here are two sorts I would speak a little to, either those that meditate to do evil, or those that meditate on the evil they have done.

1. It reproves those that meditate to do evil: you shall read of them, Psalm 36:4. "They devise mischief upon their bed." Jer. 18:18, "Then said they, come and let us devise devices against Jeremiah." There are some men that plot how to do evil, which is a double sin; it is one sin to do evil, it is a greater sin to plot to do evil. A man may go to hell for his sinful plottings, and sinful contrivances, though they never come to light. Isa. 29:5, "Woe unto them that seek deep to hide their counsel from the Lord, and their works are in the dark, and they say who seeth us, and who knoweth us?" The Lord will send us to hell for all our sinful contrivances, and vain projects, though they prove abortive.

2. There are some that meditate upon the evil they have done; as an old adulterer will with delight tell stories of his youthful wantonness, and an old wicked man will delight to tell tales of the sins that he has formerly committed. This is to act over your sins again in God's

account; this is to lick up the old vomit; this is to sin *anew*. I wish you would consider it; a man may go to hell for contemplative wickedness, for spiritual wickedness, for heart-adultery, and heart-murder, as well as for actual wickedness; a man may go to hell for thinking evil, as well as for speaking evil, and doing evil; for God is a Spirit, and he looks into the frame of your spirits. He will send you to hell for the inward lust of sin, as well as for the act of sin; and that man that repeats over the sins of his youth with delight, this man acts them over again in God's account. But I will not spend more time in the use of reprehension.

Chapter 6:
Use of Exhortation

But I come to that which I especially aim at, a use of exhortation, to implore you all that you would subscribe to the obedience of this text, that you would conform yourselves to this text, that you would accustom yourselves to this most necessary and excellent, and long neglected duty of Divine meditation. Let me with all earnestness commend to you the conscientious practice of this duty of divine meditation, because it is a universal remedy against all sin. It is a help to all goodness. It is a preservative of all godliness. It is strong armor against all the devil's temptations, and its lack is the cause of all iniquity, as you have heard. Let me commend this to all sorts of Christians. If it is necessary for you to reform your lives, it is necessary for you to meditate; for what does David say? "I considered my ways, and turned my feet unto thy testimonies." What made Peter, when he had denied Christ, repent and weep bitterly for what he had done? The text says, when he meditated upon what he had done, "he went out and wept bitterly." It was the meditation of his sin which made him do this. What is the reason that men do not repent of their sins? It is because they do not meditate on their bitterness. Jer. 8:6, "No man repenteth, because no man saith what have I done?" If it is necessary for you to love God, to trust in God, to condemn the world, it is necessary for you to practice this duty of meditation. What is the reason all the sermons you hear do you no more good? It is for the lack of meditation.

We do not meditate on what we hear. Let me commend this duty of meditation:

1. To all ministers. There are four things, Luther says, that make a minister: reading, praying, temptation and meditation. It is not reading that makes a scholar without prayer, nor reading and prayer without temptation; how can he comfort others, that was never tempted himself? And then he must have meditation. Therefore, Paul persuades Timothy to meditate often, "Meditate upon these things; give thyself wholly to them; that thy profiting may appear to all," (1 Tim. 4:15).

2. Let me commend this to great persons, to Lords, and Earls, and Kings. David professes of himself in Psalm 119:148, "Mine eyes prevent the night-watchings, that I might meditate on thy word." Verse 15, "I will meditate on thy precepts." Verse 23, "Princes also did sit and speak against me, but thy servant did meditate in thy statutes."

3. Let me commend this to you that are captains and soldiers, and men that belong to the guard. Joshua the great Captain-General of the people of Israel, is commanded by God to meditate in the Law of God "day and night," (Joshua 1:8).

4. Let me commend this to young gentlemen, from the example of Isaac in the text who went out as his custom was, to meditate on God, and the things of God. Isaac was the heir to Abraham, who was a very rich man; he was very rich in cattle, and very rich in silver and gold, and Isaac was the heir of all he had; and at evening time he went out and

walked in the fields, and meditated on the things of God, meditated on the works of God, the things of heaven.

5. Let me commend this to you that are merchants, to you that are tradesmen, that you would spare some time for meditation.

6. Let me commend this to all women, according to the example of Hanna, and the Virgin Mary, she kept all these things and pondered them in her heart, (Luke 2:19, 51). "But his mother kept all these sayings in her heart." O! let me commend this to young maids when they are at their work, that they would have some heavenly ejaculations, and meditation of the works of God.

I remember I have read of Solon, who was a great Law-giver. He says, "there are many good Laws made, but there lacks one Law to teach people how to practice all the other Laws, such a Law would be worth making." So give me leave to tell you, there are many excellent sermons preached in this nation, in this city, never better preaching I dare say in London; but there is one sermon yet to preach, and that is to teach you to practice all the other sermons.[20] Now if I am not mistaken, this exhortation will help you to practice all the sermons you ever heard; for meditation is nothing else but a concocting of the mercies of God, a digesting of the promises and the sermons we hear. This is a sermon to teach you to digest all the sermons that ever you have heard. Some men have a great appetite but have no digestion. I do not

---

[20] Consider Stephen Egerton's (1555-1621) work, "How to Hear the Preaching of God's Word with Profit," published by Puritan Publications.

complain of you that are greedy to hear sermons; but let me tell you, if you do not have a good digestion, your sermons will do you no good. That which a man is eating half an hour, requires six or seven hours to digest. I have heard of many men that eat too much, but I never heard of any that digested too much. You that eat much and do not digest it, that which you eat will turn to bad nourishment. Therefore, let me commend this duty to you as one of the choicest duties of a Christian.

Now because of the excellency of this subject, I shall desire to speak to six particulars about this doctrine of meditation in the following chapters.

1. The place where we are to meditate.

2. The time when we are to meditate.

3. The ingredients and properties of divine meditation.

4. The companions of it.

5. The materials of it.

And then I will give you some *helps* to help us better practice this duty.

Chapter 7:
The Place of Meditation

1. The place where we are to exercise this duty of divine meditation, it is said of Isaac in my text, that he went out into the fields to meditate. I do not think that this example is obligatory, that a man is always bound to go into the fields to meditate. I read of David in Psalm 63, that he meditated on God when he was in his bed. Verse 16, "When I remembered thee upon my bed, and meditated on thee in the night-watches." But this example holds out in this way much to us, that private and solitary places are the fittest places for meditation. Christ says, Matt. 6:6, "When thou prayest, enter into thy closet, (*speaking of private prayer*) and when thou hast shut thy door, pray unto thy Father that is in secret, and thy Father which seest in secret shall reward thee openly." So I say as well, when you would meditate solemnly of Christ, or of heaven, or of your sins, or of the promises, you must enter into your closets, or go into your gardens, or walk into the fields; you must retire yourselves into some private place. It is worth making note of how the evangelist takes notice of this practice as Christ did it. Matthew 14:23, "He sent the multitude away, and went up into a mountain apart to pray, and when the evening was come, he was there alone." Mark 1:35, "And in the morning rising up a great while before day, he went out and departed into a solitary place, and there prayed." Mark 6:46, "He departed into a mountain to pray. Luke 6:12, "He went into a mountain to pray, and continued all night in prayer to

God." The Scripture makes mention of a garden to which Christ usually resorted to pray, and this garden he often went, that when Judas purposed to betray him, he knew where to find him. John 18:1, "When Jesus had spoken those words, he went where there was a garden, and Judas which betrayed him knew the place, for Jesus often times resorted thither with his disciples." And what did Christ go to the garden for? He went there to pray, (Luke 22). There was the place where he shed drops of blood, (Matthew 26). There he went to pray, and there he went to meditate; the garden became famous for what Christ did there. Now all this signifies in this way much to us, that in the practice of the divine duty of meditation, we must retire ourselves, whether into a private garden, or into our closets, or whether into private walks, or into the fields. For if a scholar cannot study in a crowd, he must retire to some private study, some private place. How much more would you think to do this when you would converse with God in the Mount, when you would meditate of those glorious things of the other world? You must shut out the society of men, that you may more enjoy the society of God. It is a rare saying of Bernard, "That the bridegroom will not come to the meditating bride (speaking of Christ who is our bridegroom) but when she is alone. And therefore, it is said, Song of Songs 7:11, "Come my beloved let us go forth into the fields, *etc.* verse 12, "there will I give thee my love." God loves to visit his people when they are alone, meditating of the things of heaven.

But now I must acquaint you with two sorts of company, there are outward company, and there are inward company; now when you meditate you must not only retire yourselves from outward company, but from inward company. It is an easy matter to shut the doors of your closets, and to be there alone, but it is a hard matter to shut out company from within, from your hearts as well as from your closets. There are many men when they are alone in a garden, or in the fields meditating, they are pestered with company within, with worldly thoughts, with voluptuous thoughts, with vain imaginations.

St. Jerome complains of this himself, and he bewails it. He says, "When I have been in the wilderness alone, with wild beasts, and have had no company but wild beasts, my thoughts have been at Rome, among the ladies at Rome, among the dances of Rome." And I have heard many Christians complain (and it is one of the greatest complaints we have) that when they retire themselves to meditate of the promises, or of Christ's passion, or of the joys of heaven, they are then pestered and exceedingly troubled with worldly business, with worldly thoughts. Sometimes we are in our jobs, sometimes we are at our pleasures, or at our sports. It is an easy matter to thrust worldly company out of our closets, but a hard matter to thrust worldly thoughts out of our hearts. Therefore, when you meditate you must do as Abraham did in Gen. 22:5, "And Abraham said to his young men, abide you here with the ass, and I and the lad will go yonder and worship." So, you must say to your vain thoughts and worldly business, tarry here below, I will go up to the mount and meditate. You must not only say to your worldly company, but to your vain thoughts and imaginations, tarry here below. The Rabbis say that though there were thousands of sacrifices offered in the temple in a year, yet there was never any fly seen in the temple, which was certainly a miracle. Happy is that Christian that can do temple-work, without being pestered with these spiritual flies, with vain and roving thoughts. O! how happy might it be if we could come to the house of God, and that there might be no flies there, no vain imaginations to disturb us in our worship. I read in Exodus 8 of a plague of flies, and that plague of flies was one of the greatest plagues that Pharaoh had; for when he was to eat his meat, the flies got into his mouth. When he was to drink his drink, the flies filled his cup, so that he could neither eat nor drink; and these swarms of flies corrupted the land. In verse 24 it is called a "grievous" swarm of flies. Now these swarms of flies may be compared to our roving wandering thoughts when we are about the service of God; these flies corrupt the best box of ointment; they spoil our prayers and our meditation. But you shall read in that Exodus passage that in Goshen there was no plague of flies. O! happy are you that are not plagued with these swarms of flies, when you are in the service of God.

Question. I but you will say to me, "How shall I keep myself from these plagues of flies? How shall I keep myself that I may shut out inward company when I go to the mount to meditate?

Answer. For that, you must do as Abraham did in Genesis 15:11. "And when the fowls came down upon the carcass, Abraham drove them away." You must do this as well. When this company thrusts on you and crowds in, when your vain thoughts crowd in, you must stir up all your spiritual strength to drive them away. You must do as the high Priest did in 2 Chron. 26:20 when Uzziah the King would have offered sacrifice, "the Lord smote him with a leprosy," and the high Priest took him and thrust him out of the temple though he was a King. So, you must do this as well when these roving thoughts come on you when you are in the temple, or the mount of meditation. You must thrust them out. What that means is, you must use all your spiritual strength to thrust them out, and you must pray to God as Moses prayed in Exodus 8 that God would take away this plague of flies. And do as Pharaoh did, he sent for Moses. O! pray! "Pray to God for me, that this swarm of flies may depart out of the land." Speak to your godly ministers, your godly friends to pray for you, and pray for yourself, that the Lord would deliver you from these noisome imaginations, fancies, and roving thoughts that disturb you in the worship of God, and in the practice of this duty of divine meditation. So, these are the thoughts we should have about the place where we are to meditate.

Chapter 8:
The Time of Meditation

The second thing to speak to, is the time when we are to meditate. It is said in the text, "and Isaac went out to meditate in the eventide." It seems Isaac found the evening to be the fittest time for meditation. Dr. Hall, in his excellent *Tract of Meditation*,[21] tells us out of his own experience, that he found the evening-time to be the fittest time for meditation. And there is a learned minister[22] in that excellent book called *The Saints Everlasting Rest*, who likewise, from his own experience, commends the evening for the best and most suitable time for meditation. He says from the sun setting to the twilight, and sometimes in the night, when it is warm and clear. I will not lay a burden on any man's conscience on this. That which is seasonable for one, is unseasonable for another; some men's tempers are most fit to meditate in the morning, and some men's tempers are most fit to meditate in the evening.

Now there are four propositions, four rules of direction concerning the time when I would have you to meditate.

1. It is the duty of all those that are not hindered by necessary business, if it is possible, to set apart some time every day for meditation, whether it is in the morning, afternoon, or night. For meditation is the life and soul of all

---

[21] Published by Puritan Publications.
[22] Mr. Richard Baxter.

Christianity; it is that which makes you improve all the truths of Christian religion, (you are but like skeletons of Christians without meditation). It is as necessary as your daily bread; and as you feed your bodies every day, so you ought to feed your souls every day with meditating on your sins, or your evidences for heaven, or the everlasting burnings of hell, or of the day of judgment, the great account you are to give at that day, or of the joys of heaven, or of the promises, *etc.* Every day we are assaulted with the devil, therefore we should every day put on the armor of divine meditation, to consider how to resist the wiles of the devil. Every day we are subject to death. Every day we are subject to sin, therefore, we should *every day* consider how to prepare ourselves for death, and every day consider how to resist sin. Meditation is nothing else but a conversing with God, the soul's discussion with God; and it is fit we should, every day, walk with God. Divine meditation is nothing else but the soul's transmigration into heaven; the souls ascending up into heaven. It is fit every day that we should have our conversation in heaven. David, when he describes *the blessed man*, Psalm 1:2, he says, "His delight is in the Law of the Lord, and in his law will he meditate day and night." And he says of himself, though he was a king, and had many worldly businesses, the affairs of his kingdom to hinder him, yet he says, Psalm 119:97, "Oh how do I love thy law! it is my meditation all the day." Verse 148, "Mine eyes prevent the night-watches, that I might meditate on thy word." There is the morning-time for meditation, I prevent the dawning of the morning that I might meditate in thy word. Verse 15, "I will delight myself in thy statutes, and I will meditate in thy precepts, and have respect unto all thy ways." And Joshua, that great general of the army, though he was a man surely of great employments, yet God lays an injunction on him in Joshua 1:7-8, "The book of the Law shall not depart out of thy mouth, but thou shalt meditate therein day and night."

2. I will go higher yet: it is our duty to set a sufficient proportion of time apart every day. O! it is a hard matter to get our hearts in tune for this duty; as it is with a musician, he has a great deal of time to string, and to tune his instrument before he can play. The best Christian is like an instrument unstrung, and untuned. He has need to take a great deal of time to get his heart in tune for divine meditation. The best Christian is like wet wood, which will not burn, you know, without a great deal of blowing. He has need to take a great deal of time to kindle a holy zeal in his heart to God, to blow up the sparks of grace that are in him. If a man would fill a chest that is full of dirt to be filled with gold, he must take time to empty the chest before he can fill it. By nature, we are all full of the world, full of the dirt of the world, full of vanity, full of carnal creature-pleasure. It is our duty first to take pains to empty the chest before we can fill it full of heaven, full of God and Christ. Now I propound this to you that have a great deal of spare time, especially you that spend whole afternoons in idle visitings, and vain recreations. O! that I could persuade you to give God a visit every day, and to meditate on God and on Christ, and yourselves, and the recreations of the other world. Let me persuade you that count it your happiness to live vainly, that

you do not have so much work to do as other men have, to set some time apart, to go up into the mount of God, to meditate of the things of the other world. And that I might provoke you, let me tell you in this way a great deal. It is the greatest curse under heaven for God to give a man over to live an idle life, to trifle away his days in vanity; and so, it is reckoned in Psalm 78:33, "Therefore their days did he consume in vanity." Therefore, this is spoken as a curse; listen to this you that idle away your time. There cannot be a greater curse of God on you than to allow you to idle away your time. In this you idle away your salvation. This direction belongs to you that are rich men, rich merchants, that have whole exchanges full of business in your heads, to implore you that you would contract your worldly affairs into a narrower compass, that you may have time for the practice of this rare duty of meditation, which is the very life and soul of all duty. And the reason why you are so lean and poor in grace, is for lack of the practice of this duty. Do not be always like Martha, troubled with this and that business, but remember Mary's choice, who chose the better part in attending on Christ's ministry. I wish all rich men every day think of that text in Luke 12:20, "Thou fool, this night shall thy soul be taken from thee; and what then will become of all thy possessions?" I confess God does not require this at the hand of the daily laborer, or at the hands of servants that are not masters of their own time, and those that are very poor and are not able to set time apart for meditation. But you may remember I gave you a distinction between ejaculatory meditation, and solemn meditation; a poor man when he is at his work, may have a short ejaculatory meditation, though he does not have time for this set and solemn meditation. When he is at his work he may meditate on the promises, and of heaven, and of hell, and of death, and judgment, and the vanity of the world. I have heard of a godly man who was accustomed to say, "I thank God I can be in heaven in the midst of the crowd of Cheapside, I can meditate on the rest I shall have in the other world."

3. The third direction is this, the Sabbath-day especially is a day in which all sorts of people are too busy themselves in this excellent work of divine meditation. This is a day in which the laborer ceases from his work, the plow man's yoke is taken off, and the laboring man, and the serving man have their rest. Therefore, it concerns all of us to spend some time every Sabbath-day in meditation, to meditate on the work of creation, or redemption; for the Lord's Day is called this because Christ rose on that day, and Christ set apart that day in memory of his resurrection, in memory of his redemption. Therefore, this is your work, O! Christian, not only to come to public ordinances, not only to pray in your family, but to set some time apart for divine meditation; and may the Lord forgive us this sin that we have omitted this duty so long. O! that I could be God's instrument, that there might be a resurrection of it, that you would make a conscience effort of it every Sabbath-day. As you make conscience effort of attending on public and private duties, so you would put this as one of your Sabbath-day duties, for it is the very quintessence, the life and soul of all duty. The Sabbath-day is a type of the eternal Sabbath

which we shall keep forever in heaven; and shall not I think of my eternal Sabbath on the Sabbath? Shall not I be much in heaven when I am keeping a rest on earth, that represents my eternal rest in heaven? Let us on our day of rest meditate much on our eternal rest. O! let us on our Sabbath-day meditate on the everlasting Sabbath which we shall keep with God Almighty, the Father, Son and Holy Spirit forever in heaven.

4. And the last direction is this, that the use of the sacrament is especially useful in which we meditate, and to be set apart for this great work of divine meditation. It is the great end why Christ has appointed the sacrament, to show forth the Lord's death until he comes. Christ says, "Do this in remembrance of me." There are two things that make us worthy receivers of the sacrament, preparation before we come, and meditation when we have come. Though your preparation is not as serious as you would like, yet if you do not act rightly in your meditation, as well as you have done in your preparation, you may lose the benefit of the sacrament. Now if any should ask me, "What are those things, you would have us to meditate on, when we are come to the sacrament, or when we are at the sacrament?"

There are twelve meditations which ought to take up our sacramental-time, which I call twelve common-place-heads. I do not say we can meditate on all of them at one sacrament; but my design is to give you a sufficient matter, that you may sometimes meditate on one, sometimes on another. I will but name them.

1. You must meditate of the great and wonderful love of God the Father in giving Christ, not only to die for us on the cross, but in giving him to be our food at the sacrament. There was nothing which moved God to give Christ but pure love, and great love. "For God *so* loved the world, that he gave his only begotten Son." *So!* How? So *infinitely*, so *inexpressibly;* the love of God in bestowing Christ is so great, that the angels desire to look into it. And you that are not affected with this love, I fear you have little share in it. That is enough to take up one sacrament.

2. You are to meditate at the Sacrament not only of the love of the Father in giving of his Son, but of the love of Christ in giving himself. Eph. 5:2, "Who loved us, and hath given himself for us an offering and a sacrifice to God, for a sweet smelling savor." As God gave Christ, so Christ gave himself; as God gave himself as man, the Godhead infused this will into the Manhood, that Christ willingly laid down his life. John 10:17-18, "Therefore doth my Father love me, because I lay down my life, that I may take it up again; no man taketh it from me, but I lay it down of myself; I have power to lay it down, and I have power to take it up; this commandment have I received of my Father." Now the love of Christ in giving himself to be a curse for us, is a love that passes knowledge, yet it is a love that we must study to know. It is a riddle, but such a riddle as the Apostle himself does in so many expressed words declares to us, Eph. 3:19, "That we may be able to comprehend with all saints what is the breadth and length, and depth and height," and to know the love of Christ which passes knowledge. Great is the love

of Christ which passes knowledge; great is the love of Christ in dying for us, and being made sin for us, and being made a curse for us.

3. We must meditate of the heinousness of sin; when we were all fallen in Adam, we were engulfed into such a bottomless abyss of misery, that nothing but the blood of a God could deliver us; for there was an infinite breach by sin between God and us. This breach could never be made up but by the blood of God. That is a rare meditation at the sacrament, to meditate of the heinousness of sin. When you see the bread broken, it was sin that caused Christ's body to be broken; and when you see the wine poured out, it was sin which caused Christ's blood to be poured out; it was sin that caused Christ to suffer so much.

4. You must meditate of the excellency of this Sacramental feast; for the Sacrament is a commemorative Sacrifice, it is a commemoration of that blessed sacrifice that was offered on the cross for our sins; and it is a sealing up of all the benefits of our Redemption; and it is an exhibition of Jesus Christ, it is a *deed of gift* of Christ. God goes about giving of Christ to you and me, and all that labor to come worthily. O! there cannot be a greater feast, in which Christ is the gift that is bestowed; Christ is the banquet, Christ and all his benefits.

5. You must meditate of your own unworthiness; O! Lord I am not worthy to pick up the crumbs that fall from your table; I am not worthy to eat my daily bread, much less worthy to eat the sacramental bread. O! the thought of this will make you say with Mephibosheth, What am I, a dead

dog, that my Lord and King should invite me to his table! What am I, dust and ashes, a sinful wretch, that the Lord Jesus should invite me to such a heavenly banquet!

6. You must meditate of your spiritual needs and necessities; what grace do you lack that you may get supplied? What sin bears most sway in you, that you may get it more mortified? Now the more sensible you are of your spiritual needs, the more will your appetite be quickened to this blessed feast.

7. You must meditate of the cursed condition of an unworthy receiver; an unworthy receiver is a Christ-murderer, a soul-murderer, a body-murderer; he is guilty of the body and blood of Jesus Christ; he eats and drinks down his own damnation, he is guilty of bringing diseases. For this cause (that is for unworthy coming to the sacrament) many are sick, and many weak, and many die.

8. I would have you meditate of the happy condition of those that come worthily to the sacrament; though you do not bring a legal worthiness, yet if you have a Gospel-worthiness, God will accept of you; and the bread that we break shall be the communion of the body of Christ; and the cup of blessing which we bless, shall be the communion of the blood of Christ to you; the communion of all the blessings of heaven to your soul. It shall be the bread of the Lord to you, and the bread of life, and the cup of salvation to you.

9. I would have you meditate sometimes of the sacramental elements. When you see the bread, I would have you meditate of the analogy and proportion between

105

the bread and the body of Christ; you know that bread is the staff of life, so is Christ the staff of a Christian; bread is not for dead folks but for living folks. Bread does not give life but increases and strengthens life. So, the sacrament is not for those that are dead in sin; the sacrament does not give grace but nourishes and increases grace. And then I would have you consider the analogy between wine and the blood of Christ. As wine refreshes the spirit, and cheers the heart, so the blood of Christ cheers the soul of every worthy receiver.

10. I would have you meditate on the sacramental actions; for all the actions of the minister at the sacrament are mystical, they all represent Christ. Christ is to be read by a spiritual eye in everything that is done by the minister. The breaking of the bread represents Christ's body being broken upon the cross for our sins; and the pouring out the wine, represents how Christ's blood was poured out for us. The giving of the wine represents how Christ is offered and tendered to us; the taking of the bread and wine represents how you by faith take Christ for your everlasting comfort. Everything in the sacrament is the object of meditation. It is a rare thing for a Christian to make the sacramental elements to be his Bible. When he is at the sacrament, and when he finds his heart dull, to look at the elements, the breaking of bread, and pouring out of wine, which are all spiritual helps to raise up your heart to Christ.

11. You must meditate on the sacramental promises. Christ Jesus has promised, "Take, eat, this is my body, which is broken for you; do this in remembrance of me," that is the sacramental promise, "This is my blood which is shed for

you, do this in remembrance of me." Christ has promised that whenever we take this bread, and drink this cup worthily, he will convey himself to us. Now we must feed on this promise, and come to the sacrament in the strength of this promise; and he has promised that the cup of blessing, shall be the cup of the communion of the blood of Christ, and the bread that is broken shall be the communion of the body of Christ. Now we must meditate on these promises, and act our faith on them, *believe them.*

12. When all this is done, I mean when you have received the sacrament, then you must meditate what retribution to make to Christ for this. You must say as David does in Psalm 116:7, "What shall I render to the Lord for all his benefits toward me!" You must say to your soul,

"O! how ought I to love that Christ that has loved me and became a curse for me! How ought I to be willing to die for that Christ that has shed his blood for me! O! what singular thing shall I do for that Christ that has become man, that has left the throne of heaven, and has taken my nature, and has given himself for me on the cross, to me at the sacrament! What great thing shall I return to this God! O! that I would be made up completely of thankfulness! O! that I could do something worthy of this God!"

This must be your meditation, and you must study to find out some rare piece of service to do for this Christ, that has done and suffered so much for you; and you must never leave meditating until you have found out some singular thing. As for example, such an enemy has done me wrong, I will requite him in loving him all the more. I will do him more offices of love. To do that is to walk worthy of Christ, who loved me when I was an enemy. Then there is such a deed of charity, such a poor Christian, that his family is undone. I will do this service for Christ, I will give him some proportionable gift, some worthy gift, that his soul may bless God for me. Again, Christ Jesus this day has given me himself. He has given me his body and blood. I will go and be willing to die for him. I will say with Thomas, "Come let us die for him," for I will be willing to suffer reproach for him, if he shall call me. These are the meditations in which you are to spend your time when you are at the sacrament.

Now let me say, what rare Christians would we be if from each time we participated in the Lord's Supper, in this meditative way, and spent our sacramental hours so fruitfully! Surely there would be great benefit and fruit to us if we did.

In this way I am done with the time when we are to meditate.

Chapter 9:
The Properties and Qualities of Divine Meditation

3. I am now to speak of the properties and qualities of divine meditation. In all holy duties it is not so much the doing of the duty that God looks after, as the right manner of doing the duty: It is not the hearing the Word that will please God, unless we hear the word of God aright. Therefore, Christ says, "take heed how you hear." It is not prayer that will prevail with God, unless we pray after a right manner, unless we pray in faith, with fervency and humility; so it is not the meditation of God and Christ, and the promises, that will do us any good, unless we meditate after the right manner, that God would have us to meditate.

Now I shall acquaint you with six properties of divine meditation, for rightly performing it.

1. Divine meditation must be often and frequent. Deut. 6:7, there God commands, "Thou shall teach the words of the Law diligently unto thy children, thou shalt talk of them when thou sittest in thy house, and when thou walkest by the way, and when thou lyest down, and when thou risest up." Josh. 1:8, "The book of the law shall not depart out of thy mouth, but thou shalt meditate therein day and night." Though he was a great commander, and had affairs of great concern, yet God commands him to meditate day and night in the Law of God. And David tells us of a godly man, Psalm 1:2, "That he will delight himself in the law

of God, and in his law will he meditate day and night." Psalm 119:97-99, David professes of himself, though he was a King, and had many diversions, yet he says, "Oh how do I love thy law! it is my meditation day and night. Thou through thy commandments hath made me wiser than my enemies; for they are ever with me, or, it is ever with me," speaking of the commandments of God. He had them always in his thoughts, "I have more understanding than all my teachers; for thy testimonies are my meditation." Psalm 139:8, "When I awake, I am still with thee." What is the meaning of that? It is by his meditation of God. In the morning as soon as ever he awaked he began the day with meditation, with some sweet pious thought of God. It is the duty of a Christian, as you have heard, if it is possible, if his worldly occasions do not necessarily hinder him, (there may, you know, be necessary avocations) to spend some time every day in divine meditation. You that are Ladies, men of great estates, and have time, are to set some solemn time, some solemn part of the day for meditation; but all of us are to have ejaculatory meditation, though it be in our worldly business. There are three Reasons to persuade you to frequent meditation.

1. Because the more often you meditate of God, and Christ, and heaven, the more you will know of God, and Christ, and heaven, and the more you will love God, and Christ. The more earnestly you will seek after the things of heaven. You must know, the things of heaven are like a beautiful picture, the more you view them, the more will you admire them, and seek after them to enjoy them. I have read

a story of Necrasophus, who was an excellent painter, that viewing a picture, there came a country man by, and seeing him view that picture in such fascination, he asked him, "Why do you look upon that Picture so much?" The painter replied, "If you had my eyes, you would never ask me this question; if you knew the excellency of this picture, you would never ask me why I look so much on it." The things of heaven, the things of God, the promises of God, are most glorious and excellent things. The more you look into them, *the more you will look into them*. The more often you view these pictures, the more you will admire them, and the more you will view them. God, Christ and heaven, are like a bottomless mine of treasure; the more you dig in this mine, the more riches you will find in it. They are like a sweet cordial, the more you chew them, the more sweetness you will find in them. They are like an excellent garden in the Springtime, the more often a man goes into the garden, still he finds a new flower, and another flower, and another flower. So, the things of God, Christ, the promises and heaven, the more you walk in this garden, the more flowers you will gather. You will have still new flowers to pick. And the reason why the saints of God love God no more than they do, and prize Christ no more, and seek no more after heaven, is because they do not meditate more of God, Christ and heaven. The lack of frequent meditation is the reason why we do not love them as much as we should, and esteem them so little, and seek so little after them.

The second reason why we should frequently meditate on divine things, is because the more often we meditate of God and Christ, the more near and intimate acquaintance we shall have with them. As you know neighbors, the more often they visit one another, the more acquainted they come one with another; and the more seldom they visit one another, the more estranged they are one to another. Visitation breeds acquaintance; so, the more seldom you think of God and Christ, the more you are estranged from them, and the less acquaintance you have with them. The more often you meditate of God, the more intimate society you will have with him. As I have told you, divine meditation is nothing else but a dwelling on the things of God, a conversing with God and Christ, and the promises, and it will be a matter of rare comfort to a child of God, when he lies on his death-bed, and is going out of the world, to consider, "I am now going to a God that I am acquainted with, that I am not a stranger to. I am going to heaven, where I have been often in my meditation." It is reported of Dr. Preston, when he was dying, he used these words, "Blessed be God though I change my place, yet I shall not change my company, for I have walked with God while I lived, and now I go to rest with God." A man that is often in meditation, is often in heaven, often walking with God and Christ, and the promises, when he dies, he goes to enjoy the promises, and to be and to live forever with this Christ. It is a sad and a disconsolate thing for a man when he comes to die, to think of God as a stranger, to think of heaven as a place where he has never been. He has hardly had a thought of it all his life. I verily persuade myself, it is one reason that the saints of God are so unwilling to die, because they have no more acquaintance with God in this life. They think of him as a stranger. The more you are acquainted with God while you live, the more willing you will be to die to go to him; for death to a child of God is nothing else but a resting with God, with whom he walked while he lived. It is to rest in the heart of God, in whose heart he has often been by holy meditation when he was alive.

3. You must be often and frequent in the duty of divine meditation, by often, using it to make it more easy. There is great complaint of the difficulty of this duty. It has been often said to me, "Sir, there is no duty in the world so hard as divine meditation." It is true, it is a hard matter to keep the heart close in meditation of divine things; and therefore, you must accustom yourselves to this duty, and use will make perfectness. By often doing it, at last through grace, it will become easy. When a young youth is bound as an apprentice to a manual trade, at first it seems very hard to learn his trade; but by long custom at last he becomes an expert in it. A man that is to go up a hill every morning, at first, he pants and breathes, and cannot get up the hill. Within a little while he can get up with ease; so this duty of divine meditation, though it is exceeding difficult, because it is exceeding spiritual, yet by often and frequent practicing of it, through the assistance of God's Spirit, it will become at last very easy. Yet, the neglect and seldom nature of the practice of this duty makes it difficult, and intermission of anything makes it very hard. A man that learns the Greek or Hebrew tongues, or learns to speak French, if he intermit speaking it eleven or twelve years, he will quickly forget to

speak it. Having a long omission of this duty is the reason why it is so difficult. If you would but resolve to practice it for, say, a year, you would find it after the fact, an easy duty, through the help of God.

The second property is this, divine meditation must be solemn and serious. Though we must accustom ourselves to this duty, yet we must take heed of customariness and formality in the duty. Formality in good duty, is the dead fly that spoils the box of precious ointment. God hates a formal Christian, hates a formal prayer, and a formal hearer of the word; formality in God's service is like the plague of locusts, of which you read, Exodus 10 that ate up all the green things in the land. Formality in good duties eats up all the beauty and all the comfort and benefit of a good duty; there is nothing God hates more than formality in his service; therefore, you must take heed above all things of being formal in the practice of this duty of meditation. It must be solemn and serious, and you must be very intent about it. Slight thoughts of God will make but a slight impression upon the affections; and he that thinks slightly of God, will serve him slightly, and love him slightly; he that thinks slightly of sin, will slight sin; he that thinks slightly of God, God will slight him. And the reason why we serve God with so little affection, and so little devotion and reverence, is because we meditate slightly of God. Slight thoughts of God work but a slight heart, and a slight conversation. I will give you an instance or two of this slight way of meditation. In John 6 you read of certain men, that when Christ was preaching had a very good thought about him, verse 34,

"Lord, (they say) evermore give us of this bread." It was a sweet meditation, but it was but a short, a slight and formal one; for at the end of the chapter these men forsook Christ. It was not a solemn and serious meditation, (John 18:38). You read of Pilate, "Pilate saith unto him, what is truth?" Here is a good question that arose from some inward thought that he had; and when he had said this, he went out again. He never thought of it more, he never tarried to hear an answer; but now our care must be to be very solemn and serious in this work of divine meditation. Let me give you an example of Alexander the Great. This heathen man was offering sacrifice to his god. The priest that held the censor, the chafing-dish, in which the incense was, there was a spark of fire which fell on his hand, and he was so intent and unwilling to hinder the sacrifice, that he suffered his hand rather to be burned, than he would intermit the sacrifice. This shows how devout and intent this Priest was, even in the service of a heathenish god. Chrysostom tells a story of a lady that beginning to make a precious ointment, she calls in all her handmaids to help her. So, he says, when we converse with God in any holy duty, we must call in all our handmaids, all our affections, when we are making any holy ointment. The meaning is this, when you are conversing with God by meditation, or conversing with Christ, or the promises, you must call in all your affections to assist you, you must be very solemn and serious, and intent on this work.

I must give you one caution here. You must take heed you be not over-intent; though you must be serious, you must not be over-serious. I have heard a story of a godly minister, Mr. Welsh, that was meditating one day of eternity, and he was so serious in the thoughts of eternity, that he fell into a trance, into a swoon, that they could hardly ever recover life in him again. He was so swallowed up in that meditation, that he was too serious. We must be serious, but not over-serious. We must do as good travelers do, that will be careful not to over-ride their horses, lest they tire. They will ride moderately, so that they may hold out to their journeys end. We must be serious, but we must be moderate, not over-serious. We must remember we have a body of flesh that is not able to bear *over-much seriousness*, in these weighty meditations of eternity, God, Christ and heaven.

3. divine meditation must not only be notional and speculative, but practical and affectionate. Therefore, consideration and meditation are not only acts of the head, but acts of the heart, Deut. 4:39. Know therefore this day and consider it in your heart. There are three doors, as I may so speak, that meditation must get into, or else it is of no use.

1. It must get into the understanding, that must ponder the things of heaven; but it must not tarry there: *But:*

2. It must get into the door of the heart and affections to stir them up; for the understanding must be as a divine pair of bellows to kindle a divine fire in the heart and affections, and to inflame and raise them up, as David says in Psalm 39. "While I was musing the fire burned," so, we must muse on God and Christ so that our affections may as

it were burn within us, as the disciples hearts burned within them while Christ was speaking.

3. It must get into the door of the conversation. What I mean is, we must so meditate of Christ as to live according to the life of Christ, and so to meditate of God as to obey the commands of God. And unless your meditation gets into these three doors, it is of no use; the understanding to the heart and affections is like the nurse to the child. You know the office of the nurse is to prepare meat for the child, to chew and cut it, that the child may eat it. So, the work of the understanding is to prepare divine truths for the heart and affections, that the heart may close with them, and eat and digest them. But, if the nurse should eat the meat she chews, and give nothing to the child, the child may starve for all the nurse does, so in the same way, though the understanding chews such glorious truths, if it does not convey them to the heart and affections, it is of no use. There are many men who spend their time in meditation, as a butterfly feeds on the flower, sucks the flower. He does this not to be fruitful and useful, but merely to paint her wings. So, he studies and ponders divine things merely to paint his wings, to get curious language of God and Christ, and curious notions of sin, and the promises, but because he does not convey them into his heart and affections. He is never the holier, never the better for his meditation. But true meditation is this, when we so meditate on Christ as to find virtue coming out of Christ to cure the bloody issue of our sins, so to meditate on him is to be transformed into him. When we so meditate on God, as to love God, and desire

after God, and rejoice in God, and live according to the commands of God, when we so meditate on sin as to hate and abhor it, and turn from it, this is what meditation should press us to do. To meditate on the promises is to do so in order to close with them by frequent musing of God. This cultivates a holy fire of divine love kindled towards God as it is in Psalm 104:34, "My meditation of him shall be sweet." When we so meditate on God, as it gets into our affections to sweeten the thoughts of God to our souls, *then* the meditation of God is sweet. This is the reason why many times an honest plain-hearted Christian finds more benefit by practicing this divine meditation than a great scholar; for a great scholar will meditate to find out some glorious expressions, some curious notions. This is like a man that reads a book merely for the fine language, and a man that hears a sermon merely to make a feast in his ears, because of the eloquence of the sermon. That kind of person never goes home holier, never better. But now, the honest plain-hearted Christian meditates of the things of heaven, that he may be made more heavenly. He meditates on God that he may love and fear him more. He meditates on Christ, that he may prize him more. He meditates on sin, that he may hate it more; and on the promises that he may love them more. Though he cannot find out these curious notions that a scholar does, yet his heart is more affected many times than the heart of a greater scholar, if that scholar is not really godly. Divine meditation is of no use unless it is practical and affectionate.

4. The fourth property is this, divine meditation must be particular and applicative; for looking at things broadly and in a general manner will not work at all. The philosopher says, that *fire* in general does not burn, but rather, it is *this fire* that burns in a particular point which fires everything. A sword in general does not cut. It is *this sword* which cuts when swung in a particular manner. So *confused meditation* of heaven, God and Christ will do you little good. But if you ever would get better by the practice of meditation, you must come down to *particulars*, and you must so meditate on Christ as to apply Christ to your soul. So, meditate of heaven, as to apply heaven to your soul. This is *mine*, this is *my portion*. Christ is *my portion*. He is Jehovah my righteousness. How can I be better for heaven or for Jesus if they are not really mine? What comfort can I have to meditate on Christ, if I have no interest in him, if I cannot apply him? What comfort can I have to meditate on heaven, if I have no right to heaven. I would be meditating of a place that does not belong to me. Therefore, the greatest part of meditation is application. You must apply the things you meditate on, to your own particular situation, and that man that in his meditation of Christ can say with Thomas, "My God and my Lord." This is a man who is of all men the happiest. Blessed is that man that can say, my God and my Lord.

There are four things that work mightily on the heart in application: necessity and excellency, propriety and perpetuity. The heart is taken up greatly with things that are excellent, especially when they are necessary; especially if I have a propriety in them, and this propriety is perpetual. And I would be greatly happy if I have all these four things concerning God and Christ. When such a man meditates of the excellency of God, and Christ, and heaven, and the necessity of enjoying them, when he can add a propriety like "all these are mine, God is my God, Christ is my righteousness, and heaven is my inheritance, and my inheritance forever, O! this man is in heaven already, that can make this application on scriptural grounds. And therefore, be sure in practicing this duty, your meditation is applicative. Though a medicine is a cure-all, it does you no good unless you apply it. The water in the fountain will never do you good, unless it is brought to you by a cistern, conveyed to you some way or other. So, the meditation of God, Christ and heaven, will avail you little, unless you make application, and this is especially to be used at the sacrament.

The work you are to do at the sacrament is meditation, and in all sacramental meditation you must be sure to join application. When you meditate of the breaking of the bread, of the body of Christ that was broken for you, you must apply it, *it was broken for me*, and when you see the wine poured out, you must meditate of the blood of Christ, that was poured out on the cross. You must make application by faith, that is the great act of faith, *this blood was poured out for me, this body was broken for me, and now God offers Christ, God gives Christ to me*. In this there is the sweetness of the sacrament.

The fifth property of divine meditation is that it must be calm and quiet. There are many well affected Christians that in the practice of this duty, will force themselves too much; this is proper to young beginners, that when they meditate of their sins, will force themselves into tears; and when they meditate of Christ will force themselves into joy. It is ordinary when young Christians meditate, because they cannot find their affections worked on, they will use violence to their affections, and force out tears of joy, according to the nature of the thing they meditate on. This is just like the man in Acts 3:7-8, the lame man that was cured. As soon as ever Peter took him by the hand and lifted him up, immediately his feet and anklebones received strength, and he leaping up, stood and walked, and entered with him into the temple. The poor man never walked in all his life, he was lame from his mother's womb; as soon as he saw his legs worked, he leaped presently. He did not leap afterwards but walked ordinarily as other men; but he was so overjoyed, that he forced himself to a kind of leaping. So, there are many Christians that when they first set on this duty, because they find their hearts very dead and dull, therefore, they will offer violence to their affections, and force themselves to tears of joy. But you must not do this, the best way is to wait in the practice of meditation for God to come down, to wait for the consolation of Israel, as it is said of Simeon, (Luke 2:25). "There was one Simeon a man in Jerusalem, who was just and devout, waiting for the consolation of Israel." So, must we in the use of this blessed duty wait on God for divine comfort. And while we are waiting, God will come in, Isa. 30:18, "Blessed are all they that wait upon the Lord." And, "They that wait upon the Lord shall renew their strength, they shall mount up with wings as eagles." You must continue waiting and be assured the Lord whom you seek will come in, and you shall find your hearts melted if you go on in a calm, quiet, waiting posture. As Bernard, who was a man much accustomed to this duty of meditation, when he went to meditate and pray, he found his heart at first very dull. At last the visitations of the Almighty came on him, and he felt his heart warm. He had the appearances of the Lord to his soul, that he cried out *rara hora, brevis mora*, "it comes but seldom (but sometimes it comes, blessed be God), it tarries too short a while." O! that it would continue! Wait on God in the practice of divine meditation, and you shall find the elapses of the Holy Spirit, the visitations of God coming on your souls, and filling you full of heavenly comfort.

6. And lastly, this divine meditation must be persevering. You must persevere in this duty, though you cannot at first find the benefit and comfort that you expect. There are many Christians that have set on this work of meditation, and finding it too hard and difficult, and meeting with so much opposition in their hearts, wandering thoughts, and abundance of spiritual distempers, they have been discouraged, and laid it aside, which certainly they ought not to have done. I have read of the leopard, when it looks after his prey, when it has a beast in view, that it would prey on the manner of its hunting, is to take three or four great skips, and if it cannot take the beast in three or

four skips, then it leaves it. It is so furious and hasty. So, there is many a poor Christian that skips into the duty of meditation, as it were, by taking three or four leaps, and sees he cannot compass it, he cannot find the benefit and comfort he would, and therefore he lays it aside. This is a great fault. You must wait upon God, as I said in the former, you must continue and persevere, and go on in this duty. And I have four arguments to persuade you to persevere in this duty.

1. From the necessity of this duty; it is a duty which is absolutely necessary, as I have told you. It is the life of all other duties. Prayer will do you no good unless it is joined with meditation, *Oratio sine, meditatione est arida*, Bernard says, "Prayer without meditation is dry, and luke warm, and cold," and the reason why our prayers are like so many dead carcasses of prayers, is because we do not join meditation with prayer. Sermons do us no good without meditation. Meditation is the life of all religion, and that which puts life into all other duties. It is of great necessity, and therefore you must not be weary of well-doing, you must persevere, for there is no grace crowned without perseverance.

2. Consider the excellency of this duty, it is the soul's transmigration to heaven, the soul going up to heaven to converse with God and Christ, and the things of eternity. It is a rare duty, as necessary as your daily bread. And certainly, God conveys much of himself in the practice of this duty, as Jesus Christ when he was in the Mount, was transfigured, and his face shined like the Sun. So, certainly you that are much in the mount of meditation, you that often go up to meditate of God and Christ, and heaven, and sin, your faces

will shine, you will be taller than other Christians in grace by a great measure.

3. Study the mischiefs that come by the neglect of practicing this duty. It is not eating meat that nourishes you but digesting it. Meat may be set before a man, and he may eat a great deal, but if he does not digest it, he will never be nourished. Meditation is a digesting of all the things of God; it is not hearing a sermon that does you good but meditating on what you hear. If a man has a bandage and lays it to his sore and takes it off as soon as he has laid it on, it will do no good at all. So, when you hear a sermon, if you forget it as soon as ever you have heard it, if you do not chew it, meditate and ponder on what you hear, you will never get any good. As the beast that did not chew the cud was an unclean beast, so the un-meditating Christian is an unclean Christian. The reason why we have so many lean cows, pardon my expression, that devour the fat, and are never the fatter, I mean so many lean Christians that devour hundreds of sermons, that will hear three or four a day, and are never the better, never the fatter, well, what is the reason of this? It is because it comes in at one ear and goes out at the other. One sermon pushed out another; but they never meditate, ponder and consider what they hear. That is the reason why you are so lean in grace. You know there are many hours required to digest a little meat eaten in a little while; so, a man should be many hours digesting a sermon that he hears in one hour. God and Christ are like a picture that has a curtain drawn over it. Now a man will never judge of the picture until the curtain is withdrawn; meditation is

nothing else but taking aside the curtain and viewing God. To an un-meditating Christian God is like the Sun in a cloud; to an un-considering Christian Christ is like a jewel in a leather purse. Now, meditation opens the purse, and takes out the jewel, and looks on it. Meditation draws aside the curtain, and views God, and beholds the glorious things of God.

4. Consider, that by persevering in this duty it will at last grow easy. It is I confess a very up-hill duty, a very spiritual heavenly duty; but as a man that every day goes up a hill, though at first it be very difficult, he blows and pants as if his soul would go out of him, but by persevering in it he can go up the hill without pain or weariness; so though it is an up-hill, a hard duty. Yet if you that have time, as many of you have, you should set about this work and persevere in it, and labor that your meditation be applicative and affectionate. Let me assure you, you would quickly conquer the difficulty by the help of God. Let a man kindle a fire, and if the wood is wet, he must blow, and continue blowing, and at last he will conquer it. If he flings away the bellows, then he will never make the fire burn. But he must continue blowing until he has extracted the moisture and conquered the wood. So when you go to meditate on God, and Christ, of the Promises, of heaven, of your sins, though you find your hearts dead and dull, and full of vain roving thoughts, and you are mightily out of tune, and much discouraged, you must go on blowing still. You must blow, and blow, and blow, and at last the fire will kindle, the great God of heaven and earth will come in and help you.

So, I have completed the third particular, the properties of divine meditation.

Chapter 10:
The Companions of Meditation

4. I must speak to the companions of meditation. There are two companions you must always join with it, or at least ordinarily. I am sure that one you must always join, one is reading, and the other is praying.

1. You must join prayer with your meditation; and therefore, here in my text the same word "pray" signifies "to meditate" in the Hebrew. "And Isaac went out to meditate;" the word in the Hebrew is, "He went out to pray or to meditate;" and therefore in the margin of your bibles, it is noted, "And Isaac went out to pray." And in the old translation it is, And Isaac went out to pray; and in the new translation it is, He went out to meditate. The same Hebrew word that signifies to meditate, signifies to pray, to teach us, that we must always join meditation and prayer together. As for example, when you meditate of your sins, you must put up a prayer to God, that you may so meditate of your sins as to get your hearts humbled for them. And when you meditate of heaven, you must join prayer with your meditation, and lift up a prayer that the Lord would help you so to meditate of heaven, as to make you fit for heaven. When I say prayer, I do not mean a set formal prayer, but a short prayer. When you go up the hill of meditation, you must not set yourselves at prayer, but only join short prayer, looking to God that he would bless it to you. Luke 9:29, when Christ went up to prayer, while he was praying, his countenance was changed, he was transfigured; and

Cornelius while he was a praying, the Angel of the Lord appeared to him. He had glorious appearances while he was praying, (Acts 10). When we go up to the hill to meditate and to pray, to pray and meditate. We shall be sure to meet with apparitions from God, with glorious transfigurations. It is a rare saying of Bernard, meditation without prayer is *infertilis*, barren and lukewarm. Prayer without meditation is *arida*, dry. And as one says very well, writing of meditation, "The reason why the prayers of many of the saints of God are but carcasses of prayer, is because they do not join meditation and prayer. And the reason why their meditation is no more powerful, is because they do not join prayer with their meditation; for meditation without prayer is altogether useless and unprofitable; you must not meditate in your own strength."

2. You must join reading with your meditation; understand me aright, I propound this to weak Christians that lack a stock of knowledge. There are some Christians that are a walking library. They are books themselves. They do not need a book to help them to meditate. But you that are weak Christians, my advice is this, that you would join reading with your meditation. As for example, would you meditate of Christ? Go and take the Bible and read the history of his passion; and when you read anything remarkable, lay your book aside, and meditate seriously of that passage. As for example, when you come to read of Christ sweating drops of blood, that Christ, in a cold winter night on the cold ground for your sake should shed drops of blood, then lay your book aside, and meditate on these drops

of blood. O! the wrath of God that he then suffered! And so when you come to read what Christ suffered on the cross, when he cried out, "My God, my God, why hast thou forsaken me!" lay aside your book, and meditate on the love of Christ who was forsaken for your sake in regard of outward comfort. I do not mean in regard of union. He was forsaken that you may not be forsaken. So likewise, would you meditate on the promises? If you are a weak Christian, take a book that treats of the promises, and when you read any promise that is suitable to you, lay the book aside and meditate on that promise until your heart is affected with it, and labor that it may take impression on your soul. Bernard says, "long reading without meditation, never made a good scholar, it is always barren. And meditation without reading leads many a weak Christian over to error." And therefore, when you set a time apart for meditation, join prayer and reading with your meditation.

Now here I must give you two *cautions*.

1. You must not read much, except it hinder your meditation; as you must not be large in prayer, that it may not hinder your meditation, so you must not be large in reading when you go to meditate; for prayer and reading are given in order to meditate.

2. When you are at the sacrament, you must lay aside all reading; you must meditate at the sacrament without reading. The reason is, because Christ, at the sacrament, preaches to the eye. And our sacramental elements are our sacramental bible. Again, every action of the minister is mystical and spiritual; the breaking of the bread, and the

pouring out of the wine is spiritual. Christ Jesus is represented in all that is done at the sacrament. And therefore, when you begin to be drawn dry, as I may so speak, and you do not know what to meditate on, you must instead of reading, look on the elements. It is a sanctified way to quicken you to holiness; and you must look on them with a spiritual eye, with an understanding eye, as knowing what those elements signify, and the sight of the elements will suggest the matter of meditation. I say this because I see many weak Christians read in their bibles, and I believe they do it on honest principles, not being able to hold out in meditation, to keep themselves from wandering thoughts. This in itself is not sinful; but this is not suitable nor proper; for certainly the proper way of meditation at the sacrament is to be raised up in the sacramental elements, the sacramental actions, the sacramental promises. And therefore, you must make the whole sacramental frame and carriage to be your Bible at the sacrament and learn to be raised up by that to heavenly meditation.

Chapter 11:
The Materials of Meditation

The fifth particular in order, is the materials of meditation; and here I am to show you what are those divine truths that we are to meditate upon; this is a subject of large comprehension. The truth is, there is no divine object, but it deserves our serious meditation. Give me leave to make you a common-place-book of divine meditation. I will lay down some heads of divinity that a Christian ought to spend his life in, meditating on, sometimes on one of them, sometimes on another of them. For example, he that would avoid all sin, and thrive in all godliness, must meditate frequently and seriously of death, of judgment, of heaven and hell. These are called *quatuor novissima*, the four last things.

1. You must meditate of death; now I will not show you how you should go about to meditate of death, but I will give you some heads to help you.

1). You must meditate of the certainty of death; there is nothing so certain as that you must die.

2). You must meditate of the uncertainty of death; there is nothing so uncertain as the *time* when we must die; death comes certainly, and death comes uncertainly, death comes suddenly. There is no almanack that can tell you when your death shall come; your almanacks will tell you when the next eclipse of the sun and moon will be, but they will not tell you when the eclipse of your lives shall be. And death comes irresistibly, it comes like pain on a woman in travail, like an armed giant, that will not be resisted when it comes.

3). You must meditate concerning your fitness for death; whether you have got your graces, your evidences ready for death; whether you are a wise virgin, or a foolish virgin? Whether you have oil in your lamp, or not?

4). You must meditate concerning death, how you may so live as to be above the pain of death, that death might be an out-let to all misery, and an in-let to all happiness.

5). You must meditate how to live in continual expectation of, and continual preparation for death.

6). You must especially meditate how to be free from the slavish fear of death; there are many of God's children that live all their lives long under the bondage of the fear of death; and it is the excellency of a Christian to meditate how to be above the hurt and fear of death, and for that purpose you must look on death with Scripture-eyeglasses, you must look on death as the going from the prison of this life, to the palace of heaven, as disarmed by Christ, as perfumed by Christ, as a serpent without a sting, as a passage to eternal life.

In this way you see how you must meditate on death.

2. You must meditate of the day of Judgment.

1. You must meditate of the terribleness of the day of judgment; it is called *the terror of the Lord*, (2 Cor. 5:11). It is called by the ancient Fathers, the great and terrible day of judgment. Jesus Christ will come in flaming fire to render vengeance on all those that do not know him.

132

2. You must meditate of the great verdicts that will be kept at that day, in which all the men, and women, and children, that ever have lived since Adam's time to the end of the world, shall all appear before the Tribunal-seat of Jesus Christ.

3. You must meditate of the great account you are to give to God at that day, the strict, the exact, the particular account; it is a day in which we must answer for all our idle words, for all our idle thoughts, in which all our secret sins shall be made manifest.

4. You must meditate of the great separation that shall be made at that day, when the goats shall be placed on the left hand, and the sheep on the right hand, there will be a perfect separation. In this life goats and sheep are mingled together, but at that day there will not be one sheep on the left, nor one goat on the right hand.

5. You must meditate of the happy condition of a child of God at that great and terrible day of judgment; it shall be a day of his coronation, in which he shall be crowned with glory and immortality. It shall be a day of salvation to him.

6. You must meditate of the cursed condition of an ungodly man at the day of judgment; it shall be a day of perdition and everlasting destruction to him.

3. You must meditate of heaven.

1. You must meditate of the joys of heaven, that are so great, that eye never saw, nor ear heard, nor ever can it enter into the heart of man to conceive the greatness of them.

2. You must meditate sometimes of the *Beatifical Vision*, of the blessed sight of God the Father, Son, and Holy Spirit, and of the happiness that, that soul shall enjoy that is admitted to that blessed sight. For, because God is infinitely perfect, and all perfection is in God, whoever is admitted to the sight of God, beholds and enjoys all things in God.

3. You must meditate of the perfection of the happiness of heaven.

4. You must meditate of the perpetuity of the happiness of heaven; there you shall have fulness of joy, and pleasures at the right hand of God forevermore.

5. You must meditate of your fitness for heaven, whether you are made meet and fit to partake of that glorious inheritance. You must meditate whether God has sent heaven down into you; for no man shall ever go up to heaven, but heaven must first come down to him. You must meditate whether that Christ that has prepared heaven for you, has prepared you for heaven.

6. You must meditate what you must do, that you may be fit to go to heaven, how you may lead your lives so that you may be sure at last to obtain heavens eternity.

4. You must meditate on hell. Bernard says, you must go often down into hell by your meditation while you live, and you shall be sure not to go down to hell when you die. *Descendamus vivenles, & non descendemus morientes*, as Chrysostom says most excellently. If the not thinking of hell would free you from hell, I would never have you think of hell; but whether you think of it or not, hell-fire burns, and just because you do not think of it, your not thinking of it

will bring you there. And the reason why so many go to hell when they die, is because they do not think of hell while they live.

1. You must study the punishment of loss; what a cursed thing it is to be excluded from the presence of God for ever and ever; that is one great part of hell, to be shut out of heaven, to be shut out from the Beatifical Vision, from the glorious presence of God and Christ, and the saints of God.

2. You must study *poenam census*, the punishment of sense. For, the damned are not only shut out of heaven, but they endure endless, easless torments; you must meditate of the hell-worm, and the hell-fire; the Scripture speaks of a hell-fire, and a hell-worm, and of the eternity of the hell-fire, and the eternity of the hell-worm, (Matt. 9:44, 46). "Where the worm never dieth, and the fire never goeth out." What is meant by this worm? Nothing else but the gnawing of an awakened conscience. O! think of this hell-worm, and this hell-fire, that you may never come to be so miserable as to be made partakers of it. These are the first four things.

In the next place, to give you some more; he that would thrive in all godliness, and avoid all sin, must meditate often of God, of Christ, of the Holy Spirit, and of himself.

1. He must meditate of God, and that is a rare subject of meditation. David says, Psalm 104:34, "My meditation of God shall be sweet."

1). Sometimes you must meditate of the attributes of God, of his eternity, a God from everlasting to everlasting.

You must meditate of his unchangeableness, a God in whom there is no shadow of turning. You must meditate of his omnipresence, a God that fills heaven and earth with his presence. Of his essence; you must meditate of his omnipotence; a God that is able to do all things, nothing is impossible with God. You must meditate of his omniscience; a God that knows all things, to whom all things are naked. You must meditate of his simplicity, and the perfection of his nature; of his all-sufficiency, and his self-sufficiency; here is a *sea of matter.* What rare Christians would we be, if we did often, and often meditate on these things, instead of meditating on vanities and follies?

2). You must meditate of the works of God; of the work of creation, of the glorious fabric of heaven and earth, and you must meditate of the work of redemption, that glorious work of God in sending Jesus Christ into the world; this meditation is that which swallows up the angels and saints in heaven. You must meditate of the wonderful love of God in giving Christ to become a curse for us. You must meditate of the incomparable goodness of God in giving the Son of his love, his natural Son, to die for his adopted sons.

3). You must meditate in what relation you stand towards God, whether you stand in a covenant-relation to God or not? Whether you stand reconciled to God or not? Whether God is your reconciled Father in Christ, or not?

2. You must meditate on Christ.

1. You must meditate of the divine nature of Christ, he is God from everlasting, he is coequal, coessential, coeternal with his Father.

2. You must meditate of the human nature of Christ, of God manifested in the flesh, of God made man, the union of two natures into one person.

3. You must meditate of the offices of Christ, of the kingly office, the priestly office, the prophetical office of Christ; but more especially you must meditate of the life, the death, the resurrection, the ascension, the intercession of Christ.

1. You must meditate of the life of Christ, and examine, whether your life is answerable to his life? If you do not live as Christ lived, you shall have no benefit in Christ's death and passion. You must meditate of Christ's life, to follow the example of his life.

2. You must meditate on his death, that is a rare meditation to prepare you for the sacrament.

1). You must meditate what Christ suffered, what he suffered when he was in the garden, when he sweat drops of blood, and prayed, Father, if it is possible, let this cup pass from me. O! the bloody agony that Christ was then in! And then you must meditate what Christ suffered when he was on the cross, when he cried out, "My God, my God, why hast thou forsaken me?" When there was darkness for three hours together upon the face of the earth; when there was darkness without, and darkness within too; when there was a withdrawing the light of God's countenance from Christ. You must meditate what Christ suffered in Pilate's hall, when he was whipped, scourged, buffeted. O! what love to Christ would this kindle in your hearts, if you had serious meditation of these things.

2). You must meditate for whom Christ suffered all these things; for us when we were his enemies, us wretched damned creatures; not the blessed Angels, but us, us sinful men.

3). You must meditate who he was that suffered all this, even Jesus Christ the eternal Son of God.

4). You must consider with what love he suffered all this, infinite love, the height, and depth, and length, and breadth, of the love of God in suffering all this for us.

5). You must consider what interest you have in Christ crucified? Whether Christ was crucified effectually for you, or not?

3. You must study the resurrection of Christ.

4. You must study the ascension of Christ.

5. You must study the intercession of Christ; Christ sitting at the right hand of God the Father, where he lives forever to make intercession for you.

3. You must meditate on the Holy Spirit; and there are rare things to fill up your thoughts.

1. You must meditate of the divine nature of the Holy Spirit, that the Holy Spirit is the third person in the Trinity, that the Holy Spirit is God blessed forever.

2. You must meditate of the office of the Holy Spirit; it is the office of the third Person in the Trinity to bring us into the possession of all the Father has decreed, and the Son has purchased; to make us partakers of the decree of the Father, and the purchase of the Son.

3. You must study the divine motions of the holy Spirit; and we must meditate how often we have quenched

the Spirit of Christ, how often we have resisted these motions, how often we have embraced these motions.

4. You must meditate on the grace of the Spirit, (this will open a door to a great deal of excellent matter) you must meditate of the grace of faith, the grace of repentance, the grace of love to God, and Christ, and your neighbor; the grace of fear of God, and the grace of humility; that is, you must meditate whether your faith is a right faith, or not. Whether it is the faith of a Simon Magus, or the faith of a Simon Peter; whether it is only an historical faith, or a justifying faith; and whether your repentance is a true repentance or not; and whether your love to Christ is a true love, or a counterfeit love.

4. You must meditate of yourselves.

1. You must meditate of the fourfold state of man; man may be considered in a fourfold state:

1. Either in the state of innocence, as he was before the fall, a spotless picture of God; that is a rare meditation. Study the happiness of man before he fell, when he was made after God's own image.

2. The estate of man when fallen, when corrupted: study the cursed condition of man in his natural condition.

3. The estate of man when restored by Christ, when regenerated, when renewed, when made a picture of God.

4. The estate of man in heaven.

1. What you were in Adam.

2. What you are when fallen.

3. What you are in Christ.

4. What you shall be in heaven.

You must meditate of your sins, of your good duties, of your evidences, and of your comforts.

1. You must meditate of your sins, that is a large field to walk in; you must meditate of the sins you have committed against God, of your sins of omission, of your sins of commission; your sins against the Law, your sins against the Gospel, your sermon-sins, your sacrament-sins, your spiritual sins, your fleshly sins. You must meditate on sin to be humbled for it, that is a rare meditation to fit you for the sacrament. And O! that we had hearts seriously to meditate of our sins.

2. You must meditate of your good duties, that is how many good duties we omit, how many good duties we sinfully perform; whether we perform duties so as to please God in the performance of them.

3. You must meditate of your evidences for heaven, whether they are right or not; whether you have gotten Tribunal-proof assurance for heaven; whether your evidences for heaven are death-enduring; whether they will hold out at the day of Judgment.

4. You must meditate of your comforts; whether those comforts that you have, are the consolations of the Spirit, or the delusions of the devil. There are many men that will tell you that they have comforts, but their comforts are diabolical delusions, not divine consolations.

You must meditate of the frailty of your body, the immortality of your soul, the dependence you have upon God, and the advantage God has you at.

1. The frailty of your body; the body of man is made of dust and will quickly crumble to dust; it is an earthly tabernacle that is easily dissolved. What a rare thing will it be to take the Scripture, and study all the comparisons to which the life of man is compared? To set out the shortness of it, it is compared to grass, to hay, to stubble, to dry stubble, to a dry leaf, to a swift post, to a vapor, to a handsbreadth; meditate of the frailty of your vile body, that will quickly go down to the house of rottenness.

2. Meditate of the immortality of your soul, your precious soul, which is a picture of God, made by God, and made for God. There is no man but has a heavenly vapor within him, which can never be blown out; there is no man but he has that within him that he cannot kill himself; there is no man but he has that within him that must live forever as blessed as an angel, or as cursed as a devil. Meditate on the dependence you have on God. O! this will keep you humble, and make you comply with God's will; you depend on God for your being, your well-being, your eternal being; you depend on God every minute, you live by God's upholding you; study the dependence you have on God for your soul, your body, your wife, your children, your all.

4. Meditate of the advantage God has you at. God has all the world between his hands, as the Prophet says; and he can easily crush us, as we do a moth. As we are creatures, he can annihilate us if he please; and as we are sinners, he can throw us into hell if he please. Study the relations in which God has placed you; study your calling, your company, your heart.

1. Study your relations in which God has placed you; there is none of us all, but we are under many relations; are you a minister, are you a magistrate, are you a father, are you a master? Study the duties of every relation. Study how to honor God in every relation; study to keep a good conscience in every relation.

2. Study your calling; how to honor God in your calling, how to keep a good conscience in your calling. How to keep yourself unspotted from the sins of your calling, for there is no calling but has some sin or other attending it. O! meditate, that your shop does not destroy your soul. Meditate to keep a good conscience in your shop; that you do not lose in your own house what you gain in God's house.

3. Study your company, what company to keep, that is a great matter; for I know a man by his company more than anything whatever. I mean by the company he used to keep. Study to keep a good conscience in all company, study to keep yourself from the sins of your company.

4. Study your heart. Meditate often of your own heart, the deceitfulness of your heart; the heart is deceitful above all things, it is the greatest cheater in the world; and there are thousands whose hearts do comfort them into hell. Your heart will tell you that you love God when you don't love him at all, that you are upright, when you are a hypocrite.

Study your thoughts, your affections, your words, and your actions.

1. Meditate of your thoughts, the vanity of your thoughts, the vileness of your thoughts, the hell, shall I say,

that is in your thoughts; if all the thoughts that we think were written on our foreheads, how would we be ashamed that the world should see us. O! meditate of your covetous thoughts, of your lustful thoughts, your vile and vain thoughts, to be humbled for them.

2. Meditate of your affections. God especially looks to our affections; he hates any service that is not mixed with affection. There are several affections; meditate of your love, whether you love God or the world most. Meditate where your love is, whether you serve God out of love. Whether the world does not lie nearer your heart than Christ. Meditate of your desire, whether you have larger desires after the creature than after God. Meditate of your joy, whether you do not delight more in vanity than in Christ Jesus. And meditate of your sorrow, whether you do not mourn more for outward losses than for your sins? Meditate of your anger, whether your anger be rightly placed, and meditate of your trust and hopes, whether you do, trust in God at all times.

3. You must meditate of your words; O! what a world of sin is in our tongues! And if we would meditate of the sins of our tongues, O! what a black catalogue would there be! The tongue is a world of iniquity, set on fire of hell, the Apostle James say's.

4. Meditate of your actions, whether your actions are agreeable to the will of God or not, how you behave yourself towards God, and towards your neighbor.

Meditate of the sinfulness of sin, the vanity of the world, the length of eternity, and the excellency of the Gospel.

1. Meditate of the sinfulness of sin; sin is the greatest evil in the world, it is a greater evil than banishment, than death, than hell itself; meditate of the intrinsically and extrinsically evil of sin.

2. Meditate of the vanity of the creature: all earthly things are vain, they are vanity of vanity, and vexation of spirit; they are all unsatisfying and unprofitable; what will all the world do you good when you are sick, when you are ready to die.

3. Meditate of the length of eternity; O! eternity! eternity! That we studied you more! That we thought more of you! Study the difference between time and eternity; for time is nothing else but an intersection between two eternities. Before there was time, there was eternity; and when time shall be no more, there shall be eternity. Time in comparison of eternity is no more than a thatch-house in comparison of all the houses in the world; than a drop of water in comparison of the ocean.

4. Study the excellency of the Gospel. O! meditate of the glorious Gospel of Christ, and what a privilege it is to enjoy the Gospel; and meditate whether your life is answerable to the Gospel; whether you that have lived so long under the Gospel, have lived a life conformable to the Gospel.

Study the commandments of God, the threatenings of God, the promises of God, and the ordinances of God.

1. Study the commandments of God; whether you keep them, or not; to be humbled for not keeping them, to labor to keep them better.

2. Study the threatenings of God, and stand in awe of them, and fear them.

3. Study the promises of God, the glorious, the precious promises, the freeness of the promises, the fulness of the promises, the infallibleness of the promises. There is no condition a child of God can be in, but there is some promise or other to comfort him; the universality of the tender of the promises, your interest in the promises, whether the promises of the Gospel belong to you, or not.

4. Study the ordinances of God, that is, study how to come prepared to ordinances, how to manage ordinances so, that God's name may be honored by them. And there are four ordinances that you must meditate of.

1. You must meditate of the ordinance of prayer; you must study the excellency of prayer, the efficacy of prayer; you must study to get the gift of prayer, to get the grace of prayer. Study how to pray in the Holy Spirit; how to pray with faith, with fervency, with repentance.

2. You must meditate of the ordinance of reading the Word; that is an ordinance of God, and you must study to read the Word with reverence and godly fear, to read the Word as God's Word, to read the Word in a different way than you read any other book whatsoever.

3. You must meditate of the ordinance of hearing the Word; study the right art of hearing the Word; so, to hear the Word as to be transformed into what you hear; to be

trained up to heaven by what you hear. So, to hear the Word as God's Word, with a universal resignation of your will to what you hear.

4. The ordinance of the sacrament of the Lord's Supper. O! meditate much of this ordinance.

I have told you several heads of meditation for the sacrament.

Study the errors of the times, the judgments of God on the nation, the changes God has made in this nation, and the mercies of God.

1. Study the errors of the times, labor to get preservatives against them; it is a lamentation, and it shall be for a lamentation, there is a great apostacy from the truths of Christ among many professors of religion; you shall hardly go into a family but you shall find some or other diseased with error. Here is your work, O! Christian, to study the errors of the times, what to do, to get antidotes and preservatives against Anabaptism, against Socinianism, against Anti-sabbatarianism, against Anti-scripturism, against those that deny the divinity of Christ, and the divinity of the Holy Spirit; to get spiritual armor, to be able to resist all the errors of these times. It is a great shame, and O! that you would be humbled for it, that one erroneous person can speak more for the defense of his error than twenty orthodox Christians are able to speak for the truth, for lack of studying antidotes and preservatives against the errors of the times.

2. Study the judgments of God that have been for these many years on England, Scotland, and Ireland; the

hand of God is gone out against these three nations, and the Lord has laid us desolate, and the sword has drunk a great deal of blood, and no man lays it to heart. Now let us meditate of God's great judgments on this land, that we may know the meaning of God's rod, and we may know how to get all these judgments sanctified to us.

3. Meditate of the great changes that God has made in this nation. We have been tossed from one condition to another, from one way of government to another. Study all the changes and alterations that God has made by his permitting-providence. O! what a shame is it that we should not meditate anymore of God's ways and dealings, to know the meaning of God in all these alterations and changes, and what the language of God is; and what use we should make of them, and how we should keep a good conscience, and keep close to our principles, and how we should honor God under all our changes.

4. You must meditate of the several passages of God's providence towards us; there is no man or woman here but has had rare experience of God's providence, either in the place of your dwelling, that God should pitch your dwelling under such a minister; or in the manner of your marriage, or the providence of God at such a time, under such a sickness. It is our duty to take special notice of the providence of God, in raising you up a friend, in helping you at such a time. For lack of meditation we lose all the benefits of the passages of God's providence, and God loses all his glory.

5. You must meditate of the mercies of God, of national mercies, family mercies, personal mercies, mercies

to your soul, mercies to your body, preventing mercies, following mercies; what a catalogue would there be, if you would keep a daily account of the mercies of God!

Chapter 12:
Rules and Directions for Meditation

The sixth thing is to lay down rules and directions to better practice this most excellent and necessary duty of divine meditation; and indeed, this is the chief of everything. There is no Christian, but he will confess it is a very difficult duty to dwell on the thoughts of heaven, and heavenly things. Divine meditation is an up-hill duty; and the reason why it is so difficult is because it is so excellent. *Difficilia quae pulchra*, the more excellent any duty is, the more difficult it is. And another reason why it is so difficult, is because it is so contrary to our corrupt nature. The more contrary any duty is to corrupt nature, the more excellent it is. The difficulty of the duty should not so much discourage us, as the excellency of the duty should quicken us. Now that I may help you against the difficulty of this duty, I shall lay down three sorts of rules.

1. Rules for the right qualifying of the person that is to meditate.

2. Rules for the right ordering the subjects on which he is to meditate.

3. Rules for the right meditation on these subjects.

I. I shall lay down rules and directions for the right qualifying and ordering the person that is to practice this divine duty of meditation; and for that purpose, I shall give you the following rules.

1. Convince your soul of the absolute necessity of divine meditation. I have showed it is a duty expressly

commanded by God, a duty required of all sorts of persons, of kings, of generals of armies, of young gentlemen, of women, of ministers. David, Joshua, young Isaac in my text practiced this duty; and many women, and many holy men. Let me add, that this very duty is the life and soul of all Christianity. You are carcasses of Christians if you are not acquainted with it. It is as impossible to live without a soul, as it is to be a good Christian without divine meditation. As it is impossible for a man to be nourished by meat if he lacks digestion and concoction, so, it is impossible for a man to be nourished in grace, if he neglects the duty of divine meditation. Divine meditation is the spiritual concoction and digestion of all holy things, and all holy duties. As a man without concoction, I mean without a faculty of digestion and concoction, so is a Christian without the practice of divine meditation.

2. Convince your souls (and may the Lord convince you) of the great benefits and advantages that are obtained by a conscientious practice of divine meditation, as I have shown. Divine meditation is a mighty help to obtaining grace and increasing grace.

1. It is a mighty help to obtaining repentance; as David says, Psalm 119:59, "I considered my ways, and turned my feet unto your testimonies." It was the consideration of the evil of his ways, that made David turn his feet to God's testimonies. And it is said of Peter in Mark 14:72, "When he thought thereon, he wept." What made Peter repent? the meditation of the unkindness of the sin he committed against Christ. And what made the prodigal son come home

to his father? Luke 15:17, "When he came to himself, he considered, and said, how many hired servants of my fathers, have bread enough, and to spare, and I perish with hunger?" It was consideration that made the prodigal son come home to his father. He considered how much bread there was in his father's house, and he was ready to starve.

2. Divine meditation is a mighty help to the love of God, for, to an inconsiderate Christian God is as a picture with a curtain drawn over it, but consideration takes away the curtain, unveils God to a man, and shows him all the beauty and excellency that is in God; and it is like a fiery furnace to kindle a divine fire of love in the soul of every Christian.

3. It is a mighty help to birth in us the fear of God. O! did you meditate much of the power of God, and the goodness of God, and the forgiveness that is in God, O! that you would fear God for his goodness, and for his greatness. The reason why we do not love God more than we do, is because we do not think of God more, or study God more.

4. It would be a mighty help to the love of Christ. Christ Jesus, to an un-meditating Christian, is like a book that is sealed, like a treasure that is locked up. Meditation opens this book, unlocks this treasure; and that man that solemnly meditates of the excellency and love of Christ, cannot but love Christ.

5. It is a mighty help to the contempt of the world; for the world is like gilded copper, there is a glittering excellency in it, but meditation of the vanity of the world will wash off all the gilt, the whorish paint, the glittering

excellency that is in the world. A man that looks on the world a far off, sees nothing in it but excellency; but when you come to meditate of the vanity of the world, and all worldly things, meditation will make you condemn the world, and all worldly things.

3. Consider the unconceivable and inexpressible mischiefs that come on a Christian for lack of divine meditation. What is the reason why men go on in their sins without repentance? It is for lack of meditation. Jer. 8:6, "No man repenteth, because no man saith what have I done?" What is the reason the Word of God takes no more impression on your hearts, and there is no more good done by preaching? It is because you do not meditate on what you hear. As a Band-Aid that is put to a wound, if it is plucked off as soon as it is put on, it will never do you any good. If a sermon is forgotten as soon as it is heard, it will never profit you. And what is the reason that the mercies of God do no more good, that men are no more thankful for mercies, and no more fruitful under mercies? Because they do not consider their mercies as come from God. Hosea 2:8, "She did not know (that is, she did not consider) that I gave her corn, and wine, and oil, and multiplied her silver and gold which they prepared for Baal." They would not have prepared their silver and gold for Baal, had they considered that God gave it, and instead they would have served God with it. That is the reason why you are so proud of your mercies, and sin against God with your mercies, because you do not meditate that the Lord has given you all the mercies you have. And what is the reason men get no more good by

afflictions? Because they do not consider why God afflicts them. What is the meaning of God's rod, and how they might get their afflictions sanctified? The lack of the practice of divine meditation is the cause of all punishment, as well as of all sin, Jer. 12:11, "All the whole land is made desolate, because no man lays it to heart."

4. If you would be rightly qualified for divine meditation, labor to get, a sufficient abundance of spiritual knowledge. The reason why this duty is so difficult, and why men cannot continue long at it, is for lack of, sufficient matter to meditate on. For as I showed you, meditation is a dwelling, a musing, an abiding on the things we know of God, or Christ, or the promises. It is an unlocking of the treasure of knowledge concerning God, and Christ, and heaven. He that does not have a good stock of knowledge of Christ, or the promises, can never continue long to meditate on Christ, or the promises. If ever you would be a good practitioner of this duty of divine meditation, you must labor to be instructed concerning the Kingdom of heaven, as the phrase is set in Matt. 13:42, "Every Scribe which is instructed unto the Kingdom of heaven, is like unto a man which is a householder, that brings out of his treasure things old and new." You must be acquainted with things both new and old, and instructed in the things of the Kingdom of God, and you must be men in understanding. 1 Cor. 14:20, "Brethren, be not children in understanding: howbeit, in malice be ye children, but in understanding be men." A babe in understanding cannot be long in meditation; but you must be babes in malice, but in understanding men of ripe

age. You have need to have a great deal of knowledge that would press you to be practitioners *to a purpose* of this excellent duty of divine meditation. You must grow in grace, and in the knowledge of our Lord Jesus Christ.

5. If ever you would be a good practitioner in the school of divine meditation, you must labor to get a serious spirit. A slight-headed Christian can never be a good meditating Christian. A slight-headed and a slight-hearted Christian, that cannot dwell on things, but rove from one thing to another, cannot be a good Christian. Pardon my words, I speak them on much deliberation. For religion is a serious matter, it is a business of eternity, and therefore it requires a serious Christian; and if ever you would practice this duty that I am preaching of, if ever you would go up to the mount of meditation to converse with God there, you must labor to be of a serious spirit, as those were in Luke 1:66, "And all they that heard him, laid it up in their hearts; they did not slight what they heard, but laid it up in their hearts." Luke 2:19, "But Mary kept all these sayings, and pondered them in her heart." Luke 2:51, "But his mother kept all these sayings in her heart." A good Christian is a pondering, a serious Christian.

There is a fourfold frame of spirit that cannot stand with true Christianity, nor with the practice of this duty that I am preaching of, and the Lord help you against them.

1. A slight frame of spirit; that man that thinks slightly of God, will love him but slightly, and serve him but slightly; slight thoughts of God will make but slight impressions upon the heart, and slight impressions upon the

life. Slight thoughts of God will have but slight affections to God; for if my apprehensions are slight, my affections and my actions will be slight; for my affections and actions follow my apprehension. Therefore, a slight frame of spirit is a very sad frame of spirit.

2. As there is a slight, so there is a trifling frame of spirit; when a man thinks of the things of heaven as trifles; when a man trifles away a sacrament, trifles away a sermon, trifles away a prayer, as thousands of you do. O! it is a sad thing for a man to be serious in trifles, and to trifle in serious things! I cannot tell which is the worst, though I think rather the second is the worst. That is a sad thing when a man looks on the sabbath, and sacraments, and ministers, and ministry, and all the holy things of God as trifles. Such an one was Gallio, when he saw it was a matter of religion, he cared for none of these things, he looked upon them as trifles. A trifling frame of spirit cannot consist with true Christianity.

3. There is a watery frame of spirit; there are some men, tell them of their sins, and they will yield to you, and confess their sins, and promise amendment. There are many, while they are at a sermon, the sermon takes impression on them, but they are of a watery spirit, nothing will abide on them. As a man that flings a stone into the water, it will make one circle, and another circle, and another circle, a great many circles, but none of them abides. They are quickly gone. So, there are some men, their hearts will melt at a sermon, or a sacrament, but they are of a watery spirit, nothing will abide on them. Take a stone and fling it at a

featherbed, the stone will make a great dint in it, but this dint will not abide; though the featherbed yields to the stone, yet there is no remaining of the impression. So, many men are of a yielding spirit, that nothing will fix.

4. A rash inconsiderate frame of spirit cannot stand with true Christianity. When a man rushes on good duties, and on offices, church-offices, and state-offices, without any deliberation, meditation, or preparation; when a man prays rashly, comes to the sacrament rashly, headily, hand over head, as we say; this man is a spiritual fool, and all his holy duties are the sacrifices of fools. Eccl. 5:1, "Keep your foot when thou goest to the house of God and be more ready to hear than to give the sacrifices of fools, for they consider not that they do evil." Do not be rash with your mouth and let not your heart be hasty to utter anything before God. A rash spirited man that prays headily, and comes to holy duties headily and inconsiderately, this man catches many falls. This is like a man that runs hastily who will quickly stumble. So, a man that is spiritually rash, will run into many spiritual evils. As a man that is rash in his calling will quickly out-run himself, so, he that is rash in holy duties will quickly run into a thousand mischiefs. Peter was rash when he said to Christ, "Though all men forsake thee, yet will not I." He was over rash, but it cost him dearly. So, it was a rash act of David, when he went to kill Nabal, and if Abigail had not hindered him, he would have murdered him. And when he gave the land to Mephibosheth's servant, it was a rash act.

Consider, I beseech you, these four particulars; these frames of spirit will never make you good Christians. They will never make you fit to practice this rare duty of divine meditation. But you must pray to God that he would give you a solemn and serious spirit, if ever you would be rightly qualified to go up to the mount of divine meditation.

The sixth rule is this, labor for the love of heaven, and heavenly things. The reason why people find it so difficult to meditate on heavenly things, is for a lack of love to them; for if you loved Christ, I would not need to persuade you to meditate of God. I do not need to persuade a covetous man to meditate of his money. A man that loves the world, you do not need to persuade him to meditate of the world; or a man that is voluptuous, to meditate on his pleasures. His love to his pleasures will force him to think of them. A man that is ambitious, you do not need to persuade him to think of honor and preferment, but the love that he has to preferment, will force him to think of it. So, did you love God, Christ, heavenly things, you would be much in their meditation. And the reason why you do not meditate more of them, is because you do not love them so much. Psalm 119:97, "O! how do I love your law!" What then? "It is my meditation all the day." What made David meditate all the day on the Law of God? It is because he loved it. Psalm 1:7, "But his delight is in the Law of the Lord, and in his Law doth he meditate day and night." A man that is deep in love with a woman, you do not need to bid him to think of that woman. Where the love is, there the soul is. O! did you delight in the things of heaven? If you did, I would not need to lay down rules to persuade you to practice it. The very love would be a loadstone; love is a compass of meditation, and he that loves good things will think of them. *Cogitatione crebra, cogitatione longa, cogitatione profundal,* that is, very often, very long, and very deep. A man that is deep in love, is deep in meditation of the party he loves.

The seventh rule, labor to get an interest in heavenly things. Labor by Scripture-evidences to make out your interest in heavenly things. What comfort can that man have of meditating of heaven, that does not know he has a right to heaven? What comfort can that man have of meditating of Christ, that does not know that Christ is his? What comfort can that man have in meditation of God, that looks on God as his enemy? It is interest that will facilitate divine meditation. A man that has an interest in an inheritance, will often think of it. If he has thirty thousand dollars a year that is his own, he is often thinking how to improve it, and enjoy it. But if he has no title or right to it, alas he will not think of it, what does he care for it? It is your interest in the things of heaven that will raise your meditation of them; and, as long as you have no assurance of a title to heaven, you will never heartily meditate on it. You may know it by rote and by form, but you will never heartily meditate on it until you know it to be your inheritance. And you will never heartily meditate on the promises, until you know you have a title to them, that they are promises made to you.

The eighth rule is this, labor to get a heart disengaged and untangled from the world. A man that is dead and buried in the world is not persuaded to go up the mount of meditation. A bird that is caught in the brush, cannot be bid to fly. Alas, the poor bird is tangled up. A man that is tangled in the brush and briers of the world, well, it is in vain to bid this man to mount up in meditation. The love of the world is like the plague of flies that Pharaoh had in Egypt, he could not eat a bit of meat, but the flies got into his meat, and got into his drink. So, a man that is up to his ears in the world, cannot pray, cannot hear a sermon, and cannot receive the sacrament, but this plague of flies comes there. The thoughts of the world are *at* the sacrament with him, in prayer with him, on the Sabbath-day with him. The love of the world (pardon me in this expression) is just like *a familiar spirit.* For indeed I cannot speak too much against it. A witch that has a familiar spirit will go along with her wherever she goes. When she has once entertained it, she can never be rid of it, but the devil will haunt her. So, the love of the world is an invisible devil, and will haunt you wherever you go. If you go to the sacrament, there the devil will haunt you. If you go to the mount of meditation, the devil and the world will be there. If you go to pray, there the devil will be. And you that are in these thorns and briers, it is in vain to preach to you the doctrine of divine meditation; and therefore, let me speak to you as God did to Moses. "Put the shoes off your feet, for the place whereon thou standeth is holy ground." So, do I say, if ever you would be qualified for this duty of divine meditation, put the shoes off your feet.

You must labor to be mortified to the world, and worldly things; you must labor to get a heavenly frame of spirit. It is in vain to persuade a worldly man to meditate of heavenly things. I do but beat the air in saying this. For such as the heart is, such will the man be. If the heart is lustful, the man will meditate of lustful things, and act in lustful things. If the heart is worldly, the man will be worldly. Such as your heart is, such are your thoughts, such are your affections, such are your actions. And until your heart is heavenly, you can never be a fit practitioner of this duty. Therefore, labor for a heavenly heart.

The ninth rule is this, do not be discouraged though you find a difficulty in the beginning of practicing this duty, but accustom yourself to it. Custom will make perfectness; *usus promptus facit.* Custom will make it an easy thing. As an apprentice that is newly bound to his master finds his trade very hard at first, but afterwards by custom, when he has been a year or two at it, then it is very easy. So, at the first you will find it very hard to meditate of Christ, to abide and dwell long at it; but let me assure you, accustom yourselves to it, and you will find it very easy through God's mercy. Have you not known many a man and woman that has been by the physician prescribed to walk up a hill every day, at the first he finds it very hard, he is not able to do it, but within a month or two it begins to be easy. Those that before could not go up the hill without resting almost twenty times, now they can go up without resting at all. O! the hill of meditation is hard for us to climb, that are so full of the world, so full of vanity and folly; but if you did accustom yourselves to climb up this hill, by often doing of it, you would find it very easy.

The tenth and last rule is this, do all these things by power derived from Jesus Christ. I do not think that it is in your power to do these things, but I know there is power in Christ, and Christ will give you power. The Apostle says, Phil. 4:13, "I am able to do all things through Christ, that strengtheneth me." Go to Christ for a heavenly heart, for a serious spirit, to kindle in you a love to heavenly things, to show you your interest in heavenly things; for if you knew of your interest in them, you would often think of them. If you loved them, you would often think of them. If you had a heavenly heart, you would *often* think of them. O! therefore go to Christ, and whatever you ask in the name of Christ, it shall be given to you.

2. I am to set down rules for the right ordering the materials, the subjects that we are to meditate on. And here I shall give you in these four rules.

I. Be sure that in the beginning, until you come to be acquainted with this duty, you pick out easy subjects to meditate on. There are some subjects that are very abstruse, and sublime, and difficult. It is a hard matter for a weak Christian to spend an hour in the meditation of the ineffable and great mystery of the Trinity, or in the meditation of the hypostatical union of the two natures of Christ in one person, or in the meditation of the mystical union between Christ and a Christian. And therefore, my advice is, that in the beginning of the practice of this rare duty, you would pick out easy subjects to meditate on. As for example, I should think that it is an easy thing to spend an hour in meditating on the attributes of God, to meditate of God's omnipotence, and God's omniscience, and God's omnipresence, and the all-sufficiency of God, the everlastingness of God, the eternity of God, the perfections that are in God, and so to meditate on the works of God, the work of creation, to meditate what God made the first, second, third, fourth, fifth, sixth each day; to meditate on the goodness and mercy of God in creating the great fabric of heaven and earth. And, to meditate of the work of redemption, to meditate of Jesus Christ, of the divine and human nature of Christ. I should think it is an easy thing, especially to you that love Christ, to spend a great deal of time in meditation of the love of God in sending Christ to become man, and of the love of Christ, the mystery of love, the miracle of love in God becoming man, and to meditate of the life of Christ, and the death of Christ; what Christ suffered in the garden when he sweat drops of blood; and what he suffered on the cross when he cried out, "My God, my God, why hast thou forsaken me." Of the love of Christ that died for us, and of the persons for whom Christ died; for us when we were sinners. And, of the patience and humility of Christ while he was dying for us; and to meditate of the resurrection of Christ, the ascension of Christ, and the offices of Christ, the Kingly, Priestly, and Prophetical office; and to meditate of our interest in Christ, and how we should walk worthy of Christ. I conceive there are few that truly fear God, that are so little furnished with spiritual knowledge, but are able to spend an hour in meditating on these things. I might add another meditation, and that is the meditation of heaven; who is there that has anything of heaven in him, that cannot spend an hour in meditating?

1. Of the happiness of heaven in general. It is a place where we shall have such joys that eye never saw, nor ear heard, nor ever entered into the heart of man to conceive; it is a place where we shall be crowned with three crowns: a crown of life, a crown of glory, a crown of righteousness. It is an inheritance that has three properties, which any understanding Christian may spend many years in thinking of; an inheritance immortal, undefiled, and that never fades away.

2. To meditate of the happiness of heaven in particular; as for example, who is there of such a low form of grace, that cannot spend time to meditate of the Beatifical Vision! What a happiness it will be in heaven to see God face to face! For God is a universal Good, all good is in God; God is all happiness, and therefore he that is admitted to see God, sees all happiness in God. And then, to meditate of the sight of Christ; what a rare thing will it be for a poor soul to live forever in heaven with Jesus Christ, and to behold his face! To be with the Lord Christ! And then to meditate of the company that we shall have in heaven, to be present with angels and archangels, with all the patriarchs, and with all the holy men of God that ever have been. And then to meditate of the place itself; heaven is the Paradise of God; it is the throne of God. It is the first building, the highest building, the largest building, the best building, of the creation of God. And then, to meditate of the perpetuity of

those joys. Who cannot spend a little time in meditating of the eternity of the joys of heaven, not only the perfection but the perpetuity of them! And then, to meditate of your interest in these joys, whether you are a person qualified to go to heaven; and then to meditate how you may get to be qualified to go to that holy place, in which no unclean person shall ever enter. That is the first rule.

2. I would have you use variety in your meditation. I would not have you always dwell on one subject; the strongest stomach will loath to always eat of one dish; and therefore, I gave you in several particulars to meditate on. I gave you a large field to walk in; and I did this rather, so that you might have matter enough, you might not be drawn dry for lack of subjects, that you might sometimes pick one flower, and then another flower, and then another flower. Variety delights a Christian. And truly I would gladly have this duty not be a burden to any, but a delight to all. Sometimes I would have you meditate of the vanity of the world, and sometimes of death, of the certainty and uncertainty of death; and how to be fit for death. Sometimes I would have you meditate of the day of judgment, sometimes of hell, sometimes of heaven, sometimes of the sinfulness of sin, sometimes of the love of Christ. So, I would have you walk in the garden of divine meditation, from flower to flower, that you may take the more delight and content in it.

The third rule is this, be sure to pick out such subjects to meditate on especially, which do most of all work compunction in the heart, that do most of all stir up holiness, and provoke you to godliness and piety. Of this kind is the meditation of the incarnation of Christ, the meditation of the life and death, and resurrection and ascension of Christ. It is a meditation, if the Lord blesses it, that will mightily provoke you to holiness, and to piety, and to thankfulness. So, the meditation of death is a sin-mortifying meditation; and so, the meditation of heaven, and the day of judgment, these are soul-sanctifying meditations. So likewise, the meditation of the vanity of the world, and the sinfulness of sin; I would have you pick out soul-awakening, and soul-sanctifying subjects to meditate on. There are some men, and not a few of those, that spend many hours in meditating when the Jews shall be converted, and in finding out the time when the great slaughter and massacre of the two witnesses spoken of in Revelation 11 shall happen. And in studying out the meaning of the prophecy of Daniel, and the revelations; to know whether there shall be a personal reign of Christ a thousand years on earth, and when that shall happen. Now you shall observe that these men are very barren in devotion, that ravel out all their thoughts and meditations in finding out the secrets of God, such things as God has kept secret to himself. These men are very barren and dry in practical divinity. I have read a story of a man that studied the critical questions of scholarly divinity so long, that he forgot how to say his prayers; he could not pray. And you shall find, that those that empty all their strength and ability in studying speculations and notions, are very barren in matters of practice. My counsel is, that you would especially pick out subjects that will help you to be weaned from the world, to walk humbly with God, that will kindle a holy fire of love in your souls to Christ, and will make you more like Christ, and more conformable to his death and resurrection. It is true, a great understanding, and an acute mind, will make a learned man, but it is the holy life that makes a good man.

4. Pick and choose out such subjects, especially to meditate upon, that are most seasonable to your condition, most suitable to your relation, and to that estate in which God has set you; for these will most affect the heart. As for example, to give you three or four instances.

1. Suppose you are a man troubled in mind, exceedingly dejected; you are ready to despair, because you are a great sinner, and you think God will not be merciful to you; and you are afraid that Christ has forsaken you. Now, I would have you pick out such a subject to meditate on that will suit your condition. I would have you go and meditate of the willingness of Christ to receive poor sinners; not only the ability, but the *willingness* of Christ to pardon all that come to him. Jesus Christ is not only able, but he is willing to pardon a penitent sinner, one that comes to him for life; he is more willing to pardon us, than we can be to ask pardon. If you are willing to leave your sins, Christ is more willing to receive you than you can desire to be received. Jesus Christ would never have taken such a journey from heaven to earth, if he had not been very willing to save poor sinners. He is so willing to save you if you come to him, as that he came unsent for; the patient did not send for the physician, but the physician came of his own accord from

heaven. "The Son of man is come to seek and save that which is lost," (Matt. 18:11). Therefore, he must necessarily be willing. For a physician to take such a journey, and to come of his own accord, and when he came here, and saw he could not cure his patient but by his own death, the physician dies to cure the patient. The physician makes a bath, a medicine of his own blood to cure his patient. This is what Christ did. And therefore, he was very willing to receive you, if he had not been willing to save sinners, he could never have provided such Gospel-Ordinances. And then again, he must necessarily be willing, for he has sworn if any man come to him, he will receive him. "If any man come to me, I will in no wise cast him out." He has engaged himself with a promise; and Christ must be a liar, (I speak it with a great deal of reverence) if you should come to him and he refuse you. And when he was here on earth, he complains of nothing but that men would not come to him. "You will not come unto me that you might have life." He never complained of the greatness, or the naughtiness of their diseases; he cured the diseases of all that came to him. His complaint was that they would not come to him. Now if you go into your closets, and meditate on these things, and pray to God to bless the meditation of these things, would not this cure your troubled consciences?

2. And again, you that are troubled in conscience, meditate of the promises of God; and not only those promises that are made, to those that have grace, but meditate of the promises that God has made, to *give* grace. Study the promises God has made not only to give pardon to

them that repent, but the promises God has made to give repentance to those that ask it. God has not only promised to give pardon to those that believe and repent, but God has promised to give repentance, (Acts 5:31), and God has promised to give faith, (Phil. 1:29). God has not only promised pardon to a broken heart, but he has promised to *give* a broken heart, (Ezek. 36: 26). Now if you go into your closets and meditate of these things; they would be very refreshing to you. And then again:

3. Suppose you are in outward need, the Lord has blasted your estate, you have lost all your estate, and are like Job on the dunghill. You are driven to it, maybe, to beg your bread. You are now a poor man not worth a half-penny. If you were a rich man, the Lord has blown on all you have; this is a sad condition! Now I would have such a one spend a great deal of time in meditating of the wonderful providences of God towards his poor children. Consider how God feeds the fowls of the air, and the ravens, how God provides for the lilies. I would have him read Matthew 6, from the 24th verse to the end of that chapter, "Consider (Christ says) the lilies and the fowls of the air, how God provides for them." And so, do not be distracted in your heart, "take no thought what thou shalt eat, and what thou shalt drink," *etc.* Study the providence of God. And then, meditate on the promises that God has made to his children, to give them whatever shall be necessary for them. I would have such people as are low in estate, read the Bible, and pick out all the promises that God has made to those that need such things, that fear his name. God has promised the

young lions shall lack and suffer hunger, but they that fear the Lord shall lack nothing that is good. The Lord will give grace and glory, and no good thing will he withhold from those that walk uprightly. And, "I will never leave you nor forsake you." Gather up all the promises God has made to believers when they are poor and have lost all.

4. Are you sick, likely to lose your husband, or your own life? Then pick out seasonable meditations, seasonable subjects; go and meditate of death, meditate how Christ has taken away the sting of death. Meditate how death is a gate to let us into everlasting life; how death is an outlet to all misery, and an inlet to all happiness; that death is the best friend that you have, next to Jesus Christ.

5. Suppose you are to receive the sacrament, what must you do a little before you receive it? I would have you every time before you come to the sacrament, spend one hour or two in meditating on the sacrament, on its nature, and the necessity of coming. Meditate whether you are a worthy receiver; and what you must do that you may be a worthy receiver. Meditate of your sins, your graces, your spiritual needs. Let me commend this to you every sacrament, and never forget it; meditate to find out your sins, to be humbled for them; meditate to know whether you have any grace in truth, and to get it increased; and meditate of your spiritual needs, what they are, to get them supplied. What a rare deal of matter is here contained in these three particulars, to find out your sins by the glass of the Law? By taking the Law of God, and examining your life, and the Law together, that would cost you many an hour; and then to get

your heart humbled for these sins, and to confess them, and to have grace to forsake them. And then to examine your graces, whether you have truth of grace; whether your grace is merely counterfeit, and a shadow of grace; and if you have truth of grace, how to get it increased by the sacrament; and then to meditate what you lack, and what you would have from Christ, and to get that supplied.

The third thing is, to set down rules and directions for the right ordering of our meditation upon these subjects. And here I will lay you down *rules* to direct you how to meditate, rules to help you how to begin, and then how to go on, and proceed to hold out an hour in meditation, for better progress in it; and then rules how you shall finish and conclude this excellent duty of meditation.

1. Rules to teach you how to begin and enter on this excellent work of meditation; and here I will lay down six rules for your first entrance.

1. Be sure that you pick out a fit place to meditate in; you know Isaac went out into the field to meditate; and I have showed you, that this example does not oblige us always to go into the field, but it obliges us to retire to some secret place, whether it is your closet or the fields.

2. When you enter on this work, be sure to get a fit time, pick out a seasonable time. Isaac picked out the evening, and you may pick out the morning if you please, (you are not obliged punctually to this example) or you may pick out the afternoon; but you must be sure to pick out that time that is the fittest time. You that are great people who are well off have time enough. You to whom the Lord has

given wealth. I showed the poor man how he should order his time. We have all time enough on the Lord's Day to busy ourselves with the work of meditation. It is a Sabbath-day's work, as you have heard.

3. You must be sure of a fit subject, you must not have your subject to seek, when you begin to meditate; meditate of a soul-awakening, a soul-refreshing subject.

4. When you have your place and your time, and your subject, (these three are proper to the beginning of this work) then I would advise you to set yourselves as in God's presence. Though no eye sees you, yet consider that the great God sees you, and especially when you are meditating of divine things; for you must know, that meditation of divine things is a conversing with God. When you meditate of heaven, you converse with heaven, and the glory of heaven, it is the soul's transmigration to heaven. It is the soul's transfiguration. Therefore, I would have you set yourselves as in God's presence. This will over-awe you and make you serious. The consideration of the presence of God, will prepare you for every holy duty; and so consequently for this holy duty; it is a rare preservative against all sin; as Joseph said to his mistress, "How can I do this evil and sin against my God?" Though nobody saw him, yet he knew God saw him, (Gen. 39:9-10). And it is a rare encouragement to all godliness, Psalm 119:168, "I have kept your precepts and your testimonies." Why so? "...for all my ways are before thee." Therefore, whenever you go into your orchards, or gardens, or your closets, to set apart an hour in divine meditation, I

would have you do as David did, Psalm 16:8, "I have set the Lord always before me."

5. I would have you always begin with prayer; now I do not mean to begin with a solemn set long prayer, but I would have you begin with a short ejaculation; I would have you pray to God to enlighten your understandings, to quicken your devotion, to warm your affections, and so to bless that hour to you; that by the meditation of holy things you may be made more holy. You may have your lusts more mortified, and your graces more increased, you may be the more mortified to the world, and its vanity and lifted up to heaven, and the things of heaven. And therefore, in the Hebrew, the same word that signifies to meditate, signifies to pray, and as it is said in my text, "Isaac went out to meditate," and again, you shall find it in the margin of your bibles, "Isaac went out to pray." Meditation must always be joined with prayer. Isaac went out to pray and meditate, to meditate and pray. Bernard says that "meditation without prayer, is barren and unfruitful." Therefore, I would have you begin with a short prayer.

6. I would have you keep your hearts "with all keeping," (Prov. 4:23). Have a care in the entrance of your heart, pray to God to keep out inward company. You know I told you of a twofold company, of an outward company, and inward company. Pray to God not only to keep out outward company, but inward company; that is, to keep out vain, and worldly, and distracting thoughts. A man may easily drive out outward company; he may easily be alone. But it is a hard matter to drive away inward company, your

vain worldly and distracting thoughts. I would have you say to the world when you go up to meditate of heaven, or of grace, or of God, as Christ said to his disciples, Matthew 26:36, "Sit you here while I go yonder and pray." So, I would have you say to the world and all worldly thoughts, tarry you here while I go into my closet to meditate of the things of God, and heaven, to meet with God in heavenly things. And I would have you say as Abraham did to his servants, Gen. 22:5, "He said unto the young men, abide you here with the ass, and I and the lad will go yonder and worship." You tarry here below while I go up to the Mount of God. Now I know this is a hard matter. I am not ignorant of it. It is hard to drive away this plague of flies that pester our best duties; and therefore we must do as the priest did to King Uzziah, he would necessarily offer incense, and the Priest hindered him, and the Lord plagued Uzziah, and the leprosy appeared in his forehead, and the priest came and thrust him out of the temple. So, I would have you do this when you go to your closets to meditate. Your vain thoughts will crowd into the temple of your hearts. I would have you do as the priest did, thrust out these vain thoughts out of the temple of your hearts, or rather pray to God to do it. For, alas, it is above our power to get free from distracting thoughts in this duty. Pray to the Lord who is the heart-maker, that he would be the heart-preparer. For, when you go to meditate, God looks especially at your hearts, and if your hearts are filled with lustful, vain, worldly, carnal, covetous thoughts, he scorns all your service. Now do not mistake me, I mean if you willingly yield to this, if you strive against it, God will accept it. Let it be your work, (that is my rule) to *keep your heart* with *all keeping,* when you begin this work. And labor to get your heart disengaged and untangled from worldly things. So much for the beginning, and of the six rules to direct you in the entrance upon this work.

2. I will lay down rules for the better proceeding in this work; for this you must know, there are two faculties of the soul that must always be set on work in the practice of divine meditation; the one is the understanding, the other is the heart and affections. Divine meditation is not only an act of the head, but of the heart; and true meditation must not only be intellectual and notional, but practical and affectionate. The work of the understanding is to blow up and increase, to kindle and inflame the love of God and Christ in the heart; the understanding, to the heart and affections must be as the nurse to the child, as the nurse cuts the meat and, many times chews it, and prepares it for the child to eat, so the understanding does this by divine truths. It prepares them for the affections. Then the heart is to close with them, to eat them, and digest them, and to turn them into a holy conversation. These are the two faculties we must set on work; and you never meditate rightly, unless the affection is raised as well as the understanding. Therefore, both heart and head are the parts that must be exercised in the practice of the duty of divine meditation. Now the work of the head or understanding is serious consideration of the truths we come to meditate on; the work of the heart is increase of devotion and holiness by these meditations. Now I will speak to both, I will give you rules to help the

intellectual part, your contemplation of divine things, and rules to help the affectionate part.

1. I will give you rules for helping the understanding, to chew and prepare the things you meditate on, those things for the heart and affections. Now here I must tell you I shall be somewhat difficult and hard to be understood, this is the knottiest and most difficult part of meditation. Learned men that write on this subject, that labor to teach the art of divine meditation, do give, in nine common-place-points, as so many ways of the enlarging the understanding in considering the truths that they meditate on.

1. They would have you describe the thing you meditate on.

2. They would have you divide and distribute the thing you meditate on.

3. They would have you consider the causes of the thing you meditate on.

4. The fruits and effects.

5. The adjuncts, qualities and properties.

6. The opposites and the contraries to it.

7. The comparisons to which it is compared.

8. The titles that are given to the thing of which you meditate.

9. All the Scripture-testimonies that may be brought concerning the thing you are to meditate on.

Now there are nine common-place-heads, and these I fear are very difficult; but that I might help you a little, I will give you an example, I will go over these logical points. But I will preface all of it in that it is not the intent of these learned men that we should be over-curious in prosecuting all these logical points, for the end of meditation is not to practice logic, but to kindle devotion. There are many subjects that will not admit of all these nine. When I meditate of God, I cannot show any cause of God, and I cannot make any comparison to compare God to; but the meaning of those learned men is this, that we should not rack and torture our understandings to pursue all these heads of reasons, but we should pick out so many of them as are most suitable to the subjects we are meditating on. For example, suppose I would go into my closet, and meditate on the sinfulness of sin, then I would go over all these nine heads; and by going over them, you will understand the use of them. I would meditate of the sinfulness of sin, so that I might get my heart to hate it more, so that I might study to be more mortified to it, and to mourn for it. Now for this purpose, that I might enlarge my intellectual part of consideration,

1. I will begin with the description of sin, and I will say this to my soul when I am alone, "O! my soul! why should you not hate and abhor sin? Is not sin the breach of the holy Law of God? And doesn't it therefore deserve eternal damnation? Isn't sin walking contrary to God? And certainly, that man that walks contrary to God, walks contrary to heaven, and contrary to his own happiness. Is not sin most opposite to the greatest good, and therefore must necessarily be the greatest evil? And why then should not sin have the greatest sorrow? Why should I not hate sin above all things, if it is the greatest evil?"

2. I would proceed to the distribution of sin; and in this way I would say to my soul: "O! my soul! How are you diseased with sin! How are you spread all over with iniquity! You are guilty of the first sin that ever was committed in the world, of Adam's eating the forbidden fruit; that sin is yours by imputation. "For in him (the Apostle says) we all sinned," (Rom. 5:12). And you will never be free from the guilt of the imputation of Adam's sin, until you are by faith made partaker of the imputation of Christ's righteousness. You are guilty, O! my soul, not only of Adam's sin by imputation, but of original sin by propagation; you were conceived in sin, and you are born in iniquity. You have a nature which you carry about with you, which makes you prone to all sin, and indisposed to all good. You have a nature that defiles all your holy duties, and you are guilty of many actual transgressions, of heart-sins, of lip sins, of life sins, of sins of omission, *etc.* How many good duties have I omitted! Of sins of commission, how many evil actions have I committed! And you are guilty of sins against the Law, and sins against the Gospel. (Then I would reckon up some sins). And you, soul, are guilty of fleshly, and outward, and visible sins; and you are especially, O! my soul, guilty of inward, spiritual and invisible sins, of heart-adultery, though not outward adultery; of heart-murder, of heart-idolatry, of pride, vain-glory, hypocrisy, self-seeking." So, you have the second head or point in the division of sin.

3. I would come to the third head, and consider the original and cause of sin; and I would say this: "O! my soul! surely God is not the author of all these sins that I am guilty

of; it is the greatest blasphemy in the world to charge God with our sins. God cannot be the author of that of which he is the punisher. Judas did not betray Christ, because it was merely determined he should do it, but it was out of covetousness; and the brethren of Judah did not harm Joseph because it was merely, decreed they should do it, but out of envy. O! it is my wicked heart that is the root of all my sin. It is not the devil that is the origin of my sin, for the devil cannot force me to sin. The devil persuades me to sin, tempts me to sin, but he cannot compel me to sin; sin came into the world by Adam's disobedience, (Rom. 5:12). By one man, sin came into the world. And my wicked heart is the root of all my sin. O! my soul! You should you now abhor yourself because of your sin.

4. I would have you consider the cursed fruits and effects of sin. I would say it in this way, "O! my soul! be humbled for your sins. O! lie in the dust because of your sin;" for it is sin that is the cause of all evil; temporal, spiritual and eternal. Sin brings spiritual, temporal, and eternal curses. It was sin which put devilishness into the angels and made the angels in heaven to become devils who will go to hell. It was sin that brought the flood on the old world. It was sin that turned heaven into hell and made God rain down fire and brimstone upon Sodom and Gomorrah. It is sin that kindles the fire in hell; the fire of hell would go out were it not for sin. Sin is worse than hell, because it is the cause of hell. I would meditate in this way, "Surely sin is more opposite to God than hell, for God is the author of hell, God made hell for sinners. But God is not the author of sin; and therefore,

O! my soul, do you hate sin more than affliction, no, more than hell itself?"

5. I would proceed to consider the adjuncts and properties of sin in general, and of my sin in particular; and I would in this way meditate on this common-place head. "O! that the Lord would work in my heart a further abhorrence of all sin! O! that sin might be more loathed; for sin is of a defiling nature, of a destructive nature. Sin is of a defiling nature in that it defiles my person, it defiles my sacraments, my prayers, the sermons I hear; it makes me like a dog, like a swine, no, it makes me like a devil. "I have chosen twelve, and one of you is a devil," Christ said." Sin makes you nasty and loathsome in God's sight; sin defiles your civil actions, "The plowing of a wicked man is sin;" sin defiles the land in which you live, (Ezek. 14). The land is defiled by your idolatry; sin defiles the whole of creation. "O! my soul! Will you make a sport of that which defiles the whole Creation?" And then I would say, "sin is of a destructive nature, it destroys the body, it destroys the soul for evermore." And then I would consider the properties of my sin in particular. I would say this: "O! my soul! how great is your guilt! I have sinned not only against God, but against light; my sins have bloody aggravations, I have sinned against the heart-blood-mercy of Jesus Christ. I have sinned against many sacrament-vows that I have made; I have sinned against knowledge, and against conscience."

6. I would consider the opposites to the thing I meditate on; what is opposite to sin? Why, it is grace. Then I would meditate of the excellency of grace; and I would say,

"O! my soul! How beautiful is that soul that is endued with grace! Sin makes me like a devil. Sin stamps the devil's image on my soul, but grace makes me God's picture. Grace is the portraiture of the Holy Spirit. Grace ennobles the soul, it legitimates the soul, it elevates the soul. O! the beauty of a soul enriched with grace! O! The heavenly excellency of a gracious soul!" Now by how much Grace is more excellent, by so much is sin more odious, for sin destroys Grace.

7. I would consider the comparisons to which sin is compared; and I would say this, "O! my soul! will you not abhor sin? Sin is compared to bruises, sores, putrefaction, leprosy, a plague, the excrements of a man. And it is called in Scripture an abominable thing; it is compared to the filth under a man's nails, and to the putrefactions of sores; and the dung, the excrements of man; and will you love that which is loathsome to God? Shall sin be so abominable in the sight of God, and shall it not be so in my sight?

8. I would consider the titles that are given to sin; and I would say this, "Sin is called "robbing God," (Mal. 3). Shall I rob God of his glory by my sin? O! God forbid. Sin is called an injury to God; shall I injure my Savior by my sins? It is called "striking through the name of God," so the Hebrew word signifies, which we translate "to swear;" it is a *deicidium*, the killing, the murdering of God; and O! my soul! Will you do as much as in you lies to murder your Savior, to crucify Christ afresh by your sins?

9. I would consider all that the Scripture says concerning sin. I would consider the wrath of God against sin, I would consider all the threatenings of God against sin;

and especially I would study what Christ suffered to free us from sin, and I would behold the odiousness of sin on Christ's cross. Sin made Christ sweat drops of blood, and shall it not make me shed tears? Sin made Christ cry, "My God, my God, why hast you forsaken me?" and shall it not make me cry out, "O! miserable man that I am! who shall deliver me from this body of sin?" And then I would consider what hope there is of pardon through Christ, and what promises there are made of pardon.

In this way, I have cut out a pattern, and gone over these nine heads; and you will say, here is work for many hours to that Christian that is of a mean capacity, that is able in some measure to go over these. Here you see what rich tools you have by going over these logical helps; and as I have done concerning sin, so may you do concerning the sacrament; and when you meditate of heaven, you may go over these heads, and consider the description of heaven, and its distribution, and the causes, and the effects, and the opposites, and the comparisons, and this will furnish you with intellectual matter. Now because these logical heads are somewhat difficult, I will give you some plainer rules, for helping ordinary Christians, those that are babes in the school of grace, and are not able to enlarge their thoughts upon any subject. I will give you briefly five easy rules to help you to enlarge your thoughts on what subjects you choose to meditate on.

1. You must consider what the Scripture says of the subject you would spend an hour in meditation about; for example, would you meditate on the promises? Do you want

matter to furnish you? Take the Bible, and consider what the Scripture says concerning the preciousness of the promises, the freeness, the riches, the infallibleness of the promises, the universality of the tender of the promises, the variety of the promises; consider what the Scripture says of promises to grace, and promises of grace; consider all the many rare and admirable promises that are in the Word of God, and pick out some choice of them to meditate on. So likewise, would you meditate of the sacrament? Take your Bible and consider what you have read concerning the sacrament, its nature, and its excellency, the excellency of the feast, and the end why God has appointed the sacrament, and the way and means by which you may come to be prepared, and made fit to be worthy, receivers. And consider the danger of coming unworthily, and the happiness of coming worthily. But if this is too hard, I will give you an easy help.

2. Consider what sermons you have heard of that subject you would meditate on, and labor to recollect the heads of any sermon you have heard and make use of them to help you to enlarge your thoughts in meditation. As for example, I have made many sermons of late on the promises. Any of those sermons would furnish you with matter enough for meditation on the promises. I have made many sermons on the weekday to set out the happiness of heaven; and many sermons I have preached lately of the divine attributes of God, which is a rare subject to meditate on. If you would meditate on the attributes of God, you must labor to recollect what you have heard of this subject, and that would furnish you with matter. So, would you meditate

on heaven, or of anything that you find too hard to enlarge yourselves about? Take the help of sermons that you have heard; or if that is too hard for you, let me propound a third.

The third way that is easier than both of these is you take a book that treats the subject you would meditate on. There is no divine subject but there is some book or other that treats it. There are many books that treat of the four last things, which are four rare materials of meditation, the *Quatuor Novissima*, death and hell, and the day of Judgment and heaven; and there are many books that treat of the preciousness of the promises, the sinfulness of sin, the excellency of Christ, and the sacrament. Now if you find you are barren in meditation, and do not know how to spend an hour in meditating on any of these subjects, take one of these books before you. Now I do not mean you should read these books, but only pick out some choice things, and then muse and meditate what these books will suggest to you.

4. Let me add another rule: be sure always in your meditation, to join application. Be sure to join examination, and application, and contemplation, and consideration; this is a rule of great concern to the weakest of Christians. For example, would you meditate on sin, of the sinfulness of sin? Be sure to draw down your meditation to application, make application to your own soul, and consider whether your sins are pardoned. Not only consider the grievousness of sin in general, for general contemplation of things, though never so excellent, will not work on the soul; I hardly ever heard of a man that was converted by generalities. It is the *particular application* that works on the heart and

affections. Nathan, as long as he told David of his sin in a way of a parable, David was not worked on. He was forced at last to tell him, "You are the man;" then David confesses his sin. You shall seldom hear a general sermon do any good. It is the particular application that works on people's hearts. And therefore, in all your exercise of divine meditation, be sure to draw down things to particulars. For example, would you meditate on heaven? Apply it to your soul, and ask your soul, "Am I fit to go to that place? Do I have a heavenly disposition? Do I have heavenly qualifications? Am I one of those whose names are written in heaven? Is that my inheritance? Is that my house?" This will exceedingly affect you; it will make your meditation to be very useful, and very powerful; and so, when you meditate of death, still draw down to examination, "Am I fit for death? Will death be a happy hour to me? Am I one of those that shall enjoy God after death?"

5. The fifth rule is this, be sure always in your meditation to consider the means how to obtain what you meditate on if it is good, and the means to shun it, if it is evil. The means to get what you meditate on, if it is, if you meditate of heaven, then consider the means how to *enjoy* that blessed inheritance. And if you meditate on the promises, consider how you shall do that by which you may be heirs of all these promises. And on the contrary, if you meditate of evil things, what means there are to be used to shun these evil things. If you would meditate on sin, think, "what must I do to avoid sin, that I may not be polluted and undefiled, that I may get my sins pardoned, and my soul

purged." And when you meditate on hell, think, "what shall I do to escape those everlasting burnings?" These are the five helps to weak Christians.

6. You to whom the Lord has given understanding, I would have you fly to those nine common-place-heads: if you are able to study the cause of the thing you meditate on, the effects and the properties, and the distribution and description, *etc.* And this I am sure will furnish you with rare matter, with abundance of materials of meditation; that man that is pleased to put these things in practice, will find his heart will never lack a matter to meditate upon.

So much for the intellectual part of meditation, which is the knotty and difficult part.

2. Now I come to that which is the easiest part of meditation, I mean easy to understand, but not easy to practice; I come to that which is the best part of meditation, the very life and soul of meditation, and that is to help you to get your affections warmed and heated by the things you meditate on. The work of the understanding is nothing else but to be as a divine pair of bellows, to kindle and inflame the heart and affections; the work of the understanding is to chew and prepare matter, to help the affections. Now then I am to give you some directions and helps for the affectionate part, to get your affections warmed and heated, so as to stir up piety, and devotion in your souls. Now, for working on your affections, learned men that write on this subject propound six common-place-heads, as so many ways to raise the affections, and to get them so excited as to increase grace and holiness in the soul.

1. You must labor to get an enjoyment and a savor of the things you meditate on.

2. You must complain before God for the lack of that enjoyment.

3. You must wish you had a supply of what you need of this enjoyment and taste of the things you meditate on.

4. You must confess your inability, as of yourselves to do this.

5. You must petition to God for help.

6. You must confidently believe God will help you.

Here are six helps for the affectionate part of meditation. Now, that you may know the use of these helps, I shall go over them all by way of instance. I have given you an instance concerning the sinfulness of sin, I went over nine common-place heads, and showed you how you should enlarge in every particular about the sinfulness of sin; now I will proceed further in this instance, and show you how you should make use of these particulars, to get your affections raised and warmed, and stirred up to more holiness. After I have traversed all the heads of reason, and have considered the description, the distribution, cause and effects of sin, now I come to the work of the affections. And *here:*

1. I will labor to get my heart affected with the bitterness of sin, I will labor to taste its bitterness, and to get my heart in a mourning frame; and I will in this way say to myself, "O! my soul, is sin so odious to God, that no sacrifice but the sacrifice of the blood of God can appease God's wrath? And shall it not be odious to me? Was sin so displeasing to God, and so defiling to the soul, that no bath

186

but a bath of Christ's blood can wash away its stain? And shall I make a mock of that sin that cost the blood of Christ? Was sin a burden to Christ? And shall it not be a burden to me?" So, I would reason with myself, "Did sin make Christ shed drops of blood, and shall it not make me shed a few tears? Did Christ cry out, "My God, my God, why hast thou forsaken me," for our sins, I mean for our sins he took on him? And shall I make a sport of sin? Shall I make a mock of sin? Does David complain, that his sins were "a burden too heavy for him to bear." And does Paul cry out, O! wretched man that I am! who shall deliver me from this body of sin? And shall not sin be bitter to me? Shall I not mourn that I have sinned against so gracious a God, so merciful a Redeemer, so holy a sanctifier?

2. I would proceed to the second, and begin to complain of the hardness of my heart, and of my unaffectedness with the sins I am guilty of; and I would in this way say to my soul, "O! my soul! how is it that you can mourn for any outward loss, if you lose but a child, though it may be you have half a score? If you lose but one of them, you can mourn immoderately; if you lose your wife, your husband, any part of your estate, you can mourn too much; but you have not one tear for your sins? How is it, O! my soul, that you should be so hard-hearted, and unaffected with your sins? Is not sin *Deicidium*? Is not sin a murdering of God in as much as in us lies; is not sin *animaecidium*, that which slays the soul? Is not sin a dethroning of God, a robbing of God, an injuring of God? How is it then that I am no more affected with my sin? How is it that after so many

sermons, so many sacraments, so many years being in the school of Christ, after so many mercies received from God, so many afflictions the Lord has inflicted on me, yet my heart should be so hard, and so flinty, and so stony? I can easily hate my enemy too soon, which I should not do, but sin that is my *greatest enemy* I cannot hate that, which I should hate most of all! I must love my outward enemy, but God bids me hate my sin. God does not bid me to love the devil, or the works of the devil. I can hate that which I should love, but I cannot hate that which I should hate. I cannot hate my sin."

3. I would proceed to stir up my affections to a passionate wish; and I would say to my soul in this way, "O! that my heart was more soft. O! that I could mourn with a godly mourning, not with a legal mourning, but with a mourning that is out of love to God. O! that I could mourn with repentance to life, with a Gospel-sorrow for all my sins of omission, commission, my sacrament-sins, my family-sins, my closet-sins, the sins of my youth, the sins of my riper age, for all my unkindness against my God: O! that my head were waters, and mine eyes a fountain of tears, that I could mourn day and night for my sins, and the sins of the times, and the sins of the place wherein I live. O! that rivers of tears would run down my eyes, because I have sinned against my God!" In this way would I wish, and passionately express myself, so that I might get my heart raised up. "O! that the Lord would pour down the spirit of mourning upon me."

4. I would make a humble confession of my own inability, to mourn; and I would say this, "O Lord! you know it is not in man to direct his own ways, it is not in man to

guide his own steps; I know, O! Lord, that I am not able of myself to think a good thought; it is easier for me to cleave a rock in pieces, than to cleave my rocky heart by my own strength. There must be an Almighty power to get my heart soft; for my heart, O! Lord is harder than the millstone, and I cannot soften it. I would mourn that I cannot mourn, that I do not have the power; I can do nothing without power derived from Jesus Christ."

5. I would go to supplication after confession, and I would petition to God for strength; and I would say, "O! Lord! you that have promised to take away my heart of stone, and give me a heart of flesh, have you not promised to work all my works in me, and for me? Have you not promised "to subdue my iniquities?" (Micah 7:19). Have you not promised that sin shall not have dominion over me? This is the promise, (Rom. 6). Now Lord, you have promised these things, I ask you that you perform these promises. You are the God of Truth, and so, make good your word, take away my heart of stone, and give me the ability to mourn for my great abominations. And work this work in me and for me; and subdue my iniquities, and do not let sin have dominion over me. Rather give me over to the dominion of men. Though I would not be a slave to men, yet I had rather be a slave to all the men in the world, yes, a slave to the Turk, than a slave to the devil. I would rather be a galley-slave than a devil's-slave; of all slavery, Lord, deliver me from soul-slavery." And in this way, I would supplicate and petition God; and when I have done all *this:*

6. I would encourage myself by faith in a confident hope and trust in God, that the Lord will hear my prayer, and give me strength against my corruptions, and supply me with help in all my necessities; and I would say this, "O! Lord, you have promised that whatever I ask in the name of Christ, shall be granted to me; blessed God! I ask this day in the name of Christ for the pardon of sin, and power against sin, and a broken heart for sin, and from sin. I ask repentance to salvation; you have promised to give it, I believe you will give it; I believe, Lord, help my unbelief. And then I would say to my soul, why are you disquieted, "O! my soul? why are you cast down? Why are you troubled? Still trust in God, depend on God, for he is my help, he is my joy, in him will I put my trust."

In this way, I have gone over these six heads, and I have given you one instance. Now, I would have you know, whatsoever I have said of sin, I can go over any subject no matter what it is. Suppose I would meditate on heaven. After I have meditated of the joys and excellencies of heaven, and all those particulars in the intellectual part; then, to work on my affections, I would labor to get my heart affected with the joys of heaven, and then I would complain that I am no more affected with those joys, and with the Beatific Vision, and the rare company that I shall there enjoy. And then I would passionately wish, "O! that my heart were more heavenly; O! that I could taste more of those everlasting joys, that the Lord would come down and *heavenlize me*," and then I would confess my inability of myself, and I would supplicate for help, and I would confidently believe that the Lord will send down heaven into my heart, and the joys of it, before I come there.

That which I say of the sinfulness of sin, you may make use of in all other subjects that you meditate on. So much for the rules and directions, for the better helping you to proceed and go on in the duty of meditation.

3. Now there remains only some Rules for the conclusion of all this. When you have begun and entered upon this duty, and made a progress in it, when you come to make a conclusion, shut up your meditation of divine things with thankfulness, with resolution, and with recommendation of your soul to God.

1. I say, conclude with thankfulness; lift up your heart to God, and bless his name that has enlarged your soul, and enabled you to spend an hour in meditation of holy things; especially if you find your hearts affected with what you meditate on, if you have gotten from the intellectual part into the affectionate part. If you have gotten your souls raised up. As for example, if you have been meditating of heaven, and you find a heavenly frame fashioned in you, you find a desire to be with the Lord, and you find some assurance that your name is written there, and some manifestations of God to your souls, O! then close up all with a, "Hallelujah, blessed be the Lord for the assistance of this hour." So likewise, have you been meditating of sin, and find at the conclusion, that your heart is somewhat soft, and begins to mourn for your sin, and you are troubled that you have offended your God; and the Lord has fashioned in you some confidence, some spiritual assurance that your sins

shall be mortified, and that the Lord will keep you that your sin shall not have dominion over you? Then conclude with a "Hallelujah," lift up your heart, and bless the Lord for his assistance. I might likewise add, when you have been meditating on the promises, or of death, whatever the subject you are meditating on is, if the Lord has fashioned you to have a heart above the fear of death, by meditating of death, and you have learned to be willing and ready to die; O! bless the Lord for his assistance.

2. I would have you close with a resolution of heart, to spend your life as becomes one that has been meditating of holy and heavenly things. For example, "I have been meditating of the promises, I will shut up my meditation with resolution, by the grace of God, to live more on the promises than ever I have done; I have lived too much on the creature, but now I will live more on God, and his promises. I will close up with a resolution, by the power of my God, to study my interest in the promises more, and suck out the sweetness of them more; and to be more acquainted with the freeness, and the fullness, and riches, and preciousness of them." And so, would you meditate of heaven? I would conclude with a resolution, that I would labor to live more heavenly, and walk as becomes one that looks to live with Christ forever in heaven. You must know these spiritual resolutions are *spiritualia vincula obedientiae*, they are spiritual bonds to tie the soul fast to God. As the beast was tied to the horns of the altar in the old Law, that was to be sacrificed, so these blessed vows and resolutions are heavenly cords to tie the soul faster to God; and that is the

reason why in the sacrament we renew our vows and resolutions. As God renews his engagements to us, so do we renew our engagements to God at every sacrament. Now, I would have you close up your meditation by binding your souls faster to God, in a holy resolution. Divine resolution is the spiritual hedge of the soul (as one said) to keep the soul from breaking out into ungodly courses.

3. Shut up all this with a short commendation of yourself, your body, your soul, your wife, your children, (if you have any) your estate, all that you have, recommend them to your God; shut up all this with a sweet resignation of yourself, and all your affairs, and all your ways. As David says, "Commit your ways unto the Lord," and so, commit yourselves and your affairs, all that you are, all that you have, into the hands of the Lord, as a faithful Creator, and a merciful Redeemer. I would have you close up all with a committing, and a submitting; committing your ways to God, submitting to God in all his ways; purposing to live to his glory, and to walk worthy of that heavenly calling to which you are called. And in this way, I have put an end to this subject of divine meditation. Now what remains but to persuade you to the practice of these things?

That which a learned man who has written a tract called, The Art of divine Meditation, closes his Book with, let me close this with. He says, "O! that my words were as so many gourds to quicken up the dead, and dull, and drowsy hearts of Christians, to a conscientious practice of this excellent duty of divine meditation!"

It is a strange use of words he uses, for he says, "I will give any man leave to curse me on his death bed, if he does not then acknowledge, that those hours that he has spent in divine meditation, have been the best hours that he has spent in all his life, if he does not then confess he is sorrowful that he spent no more hours in so blessed a work. I am sure, when you lie upon your death bed, this will be your comfort: "Lord, I have been often in heaven in meditation, and now I am going to that place that I am acquainted with." O! my God! I have been often with you in the Mount, I have been often meditating of you. O! my blessed Savior! You are no stranger to me; I have been often meditating of Christ. O! what comfort will this be to you when you lie on your death beds! I will not say, curse me if you do not find this true; but I will say, this is as sure as the Word of God is true, you will find it so."

Chapter 13:
The Conclusion

There are four things I will conclude this discourse with.

1. I would humbly beseech you, that you would mourn before God that you have lived so many years in the school of Christ and have been no more acquainted with this duty of divine meditation. I believe there are very many that have been long standers in Christ's school, that never yet practiced this duty of divine meditation, that never were half an hour together in the Mount of God solemnly and seriously. Now I implore you, mourn before the Lord, that we have been no more acquainted with this blessed and heavenly duty.

2. Let us mourn before the Lord that we have misplaced our meditation. The heart of man is restless, it is like the weight of a clock, that will never leave going down, as long as it is wound up; the heart of man will always be meditating of something or other. Like mill stones, if they once grind, they will grind one another. The heart of man will always be grinding, always musing, always meditating on something or other. Now, mourn before God heartily, and go into your closets and bemoan it, that you have ground chaff to your immortal souls your whole life; that you have spent your days in meditating what to eat, and what to drink, and what to be clothed with, and how to grow rich, and how to manage your trading, and your calling, how to thrive in the world, how to get such

preferments. You have been meditating your whole lives long on vain things, and have not meditated on the things of eternity, those things that most concern you. You have been meditating on trifles, on things that will not profit at the hour of death and forgot to meditate of those things that are of eternal concern. Our Savior Christ complains of those men in Matthew 6, "Take no thought for your lives, what you shall eat, and what you shall drink, nor for your body what you shall put on," as if he should say, why do you spend all your time in taking thought of eating, and drinking, and clothing, and outward things? "Which of you (he says) can by taking thought add one cubit to your stature?" All your musing and meditating of them is vain. Can a dwarf by thinking he is a dwarf, make himself taller? It is not all your musing and your meditating of these outward things, I mean your inordinate meditating, that will give you some advantage. I grant tradesmen must have time to meditate of worldly things. I will not lay heavier burdens than the Scripture lays. But when you ravel away all your time in meditating on earthly things, and are never serious in the meditation of heavenly things, this I would have you mourn for; you that are old people, and have been many years professors of Religion. O! mourn that you have wasted your intellectual faculty, that you have wasted that glorious faculty of soul, your understanding, in such vain and trifling things; no, are there not some that do not only meditate of vain things, but spend many hours in meditating on vile things? These devise mischief on their beds, and meditate how to trick their neighbors, how to be revenged on their neighbor, how to do mischief, how to compass about their wicked designs? Are there not some that meditate to do evil, and rejoice in the meditation of evil when they have done it? Many old men meditate with joy of their youthful vanities, and wickedness committed in their youth, they chew over their wicked ways with delight, which we call *contemplative wickedness.* O! let us bewail and bemoan it before God, that we have squandered away our immortal souls, by exercising the glorious faculty of the understanding in such poor trifling things. It may be lustful, revengeful, vile, wicked thoughts, either in doing that which is evil, or in meditating on the evil we have done; instead of mourning for it, we are rejoicing in it.

3. I would persuade you to study the necessity, the excellency, the usefulness, and profitableness of divine meditation; let me tell you in this conclusion, this duty is not only a duty, but the quintessence and marrow of all other duties. There is no duty that will make an impression on your souls without the practice of this duty; it is the very life and soul of Christianity, without which a Christian is but the carcass of a Christian. I have showed, that the lack of divine meditation is the cause of all sin, and all punishment. I have showed you, that the practice of meditation will help to obtain grace, and increase grace, and resist the devil and all his temptations.

4. Let me persuade you all, that you would put this duty into practice; especially you that are rich people, gentlemen, merchants, and others. You that have estates, you that are gentlemen, may spare time from your sports;

and you that are rich merchants and others, may take time from your outward occasions. O! let me intreat you that you would take some spare-time every day, to go up to the Mount of God, to meditate of some of those subjects that I have propounded to you, whether it be death, or hell, or heaven, or judgment, or sin, or Christ, or God, or the vanity of the world, whatever the subject is, that is holy and heavenly. I will not lay burdens on you, I know there may be such occasions that you cannot; but ordinarily that you would as often as you can, make conscience to accustom yourselves to this necessary and long-neglected duty of divine meditation.

Let me tell you, you would be tall Christians in grace if you did accustom yourselves to this duty; the reason why you are such dwarfs in Christianity, and so unacquainted with God, and the promises, and Christ, and heaven, is for the lack of the practice of this duty; this is the reason why you creep upon the ground, and are so poor in grace, and so lean in Religion. Therefore, let me intreat you, especially you whose happiness is that you need not work every day to provide for your families; the Lord has given you an estate, and you may spare time; O! let it not be said at the day of judgment, that you lost heaven for the lack of the practicing this duty of divine meditation!

And then you that are poor people and cannot find time; you that are servants and apprentices, that have no time, remember what I said concerning occasional meditation. I showed you how you might meditate when you were about your worldly business. There is no lawful calling that a man can be in, but if he has a heavenly heart, he may *heavenlize* that calling, he may take occasion (as Christ takes occasion to *heavenlize* his discourse from outward things) to raise heavenly discourse. When you are at work, you may be by divine meditation in heaven. But let me persuade you all on the Sabbath-day, (though you have no time on the week-day for set, solemn meditation; yet then you have time for occasional meditation, for on the Sabbath all your work ceases) that is the day that God has set a part for public service, and private meditation; meditation on the work of creation, and the work of redemption; it is a great work we are to do on the day of our rest, to meditate of our eternal rest in heaven. Therefore, let me persuade you to spend some time on the Sabbath-day on meditation, but especially on the sacrament-days. There are Twelve meditations I propounded to meditate on upon the sacrament, and I chose this subject to help you with sacramental meditation; it has pleased God to carry me out further in the handling of it than ever I thought. The Lord give a blessing to it.

FINIS

Other Works Published by Puritan Publications on Godly Meditation

The Whole Duty of Divine Meditation by Richard Allestree (1619-1681)

A Treatise of Divine Meditation by John Ball (1585-1640)

Instructions for the Art of Divine Meditation by Thomas White (d. 1672)

The Spiritual Chemyst, or Divine Meditations on Several Subjects by William Spurstowe (1605-1666)

The Christian's Desire to See God Face to Face by Richard Sibbes (1577–1635)

How to Serve God in Private and Public Worship by John Jackson (1600-1648)

The Reformed Apprentice Volume 4: A Workbook on Private Devotions by C. Matthew McMahon

A Discourse on Self-Examination by Nathaniel Vincent (1639-1697)

The Saint's Spiritual Delight, and a Christian on the Mount by Thomas Watson (1620-1686)

A Treatise on Heavenly Mindedness by Thomas Jollie (1629-1703)

The Rules of a Holy Life by Nicholas Byfield (1579–1622)

The Wells of Salvation Opened by William Spurstowe (1605-1666)

www.ingramcontent.com/pod-product-compliance
Lightning Source LLC
Chambersburg PA
CBHW030828090426
42737CB00009B/922